A Biblical Standard For Evangelists

Billy Graham

World Wide
PUBLICATIONS
Minneapolis, MN 55403

ACKNOWLEDGMENTS

Unless otherwise indicated, Bible verses are taken from The Holy Bible, King James Version. Bible verses marked NIV are taken from The Holy Bible, New International Version, copyright © 1978 International Bible Society, East Brunswick, New Jersey. Bible verses marked NKJV are taken from The Holy Bible, New King James Version, copyright © 1979, 1980, 1982 Thomas Nelson, Inc., Nashville, Tennessee. Bible verses marked TLB are taken from *The Living Bible*, copyright © 1971 Tyndale House Publishers, Wheaton, Illinois. Bible verses marked RSV are taken from the Revised Standard Version Bible, copyrighted 1946, 1952, © 1971, 1973 National Council of the Churches of Christ in the U.S.A., New York. Bible verses marked NEB are taken from The New English Bible, © The Delegates of the Oxford University Press and The Syndics of the Cambridge University Press 1961, 1970, Oxford and Cambridge, England. Used by permission.

Selections are used by permission
Introduction
1. Clause 4, in The Lausanne Covenant, ©1974 World Wide Publications, Minneapolis, Minnesota.
Affirmation I
1. Clause 2, in The Lausanne Covenant, ©1974 World Wide Publications, Minneapolis, Minnesota.
Affirmation V
1. Clause 4, in The Lausanne Covenant, ©1974 World Wide Publications, Minneapolis, Minnesota.
Affirmation IX
1. *Manna in the Morning*, by Stephen F. Olford, ©Stephen F. Olford, revised edition 1983, Encounter Ministries, Inc., Wheaton, Illinois, p. 10.
2. Ibid., pp. 2-5.

Library of Congress Catalog Card Number 84-051639
ISBN 0-89066-057-3

A Biblical Standard for Evangelists, by Billy Graham, © 1984 Billy Graham Evangelistic Association, published by World Wide Publications, 1303 Hennepin Avenue, Minneapolis, Minnesota 55403.

Printed in the United States of America

CONTENTS

Introduction 1

Affirmation I 11
Affirmation II 23
Affirmation III 31
Affirmation IV 41
Affirmation V 49
Affirmation VI 57
Affirmation VII 65
Affirmation VIII 73
Affirmation IX 81
Affirmation X 89
Affirmation XI 95
Affirmation XII 103
Affirmation XIII 109
Affirmation XIV 115
Affirmation XV 121

INTRODUCTION

The International Conference for Itinerant Evangelists — Amsterdam '83 — was not only a special milestone in my ministry, but a historic Conference. It was the first time in history that such a Conference had ever been held. At its climax there was a solemn act of commitment. Fellow-evangelists from every continent of the world and I rededicated ourselves to the service of our Lord and Master Jesus Christ, using the meaningful words of what we called "The Amsterdam Affirmations."

These fifteen points provide a biblical standard for those whom God sets apart to "do the work of an evangelist." But, more than that, they have relevance to the whole family of God, for we are all called to be His witnesses. That is why this commentary has been prepared for wider circulation.

But let me backtrack for a moment. Many years ago God gave me a vision of bringing together evangelists from all parts of the world for a conference. At that time it would have been impossible. I was far too young. Some of the older and more experienced evangelists may have resented my initiative. The idea never left me, and I never doubted that some day it would happen. It was simply a question of being sensitive to God's timing for such an event. As we look back, we can sense His guidance in every step toward it.

Meanwhile, the Billy Graham Evangelistic Association had organized and financed other events of a similar nature. There was the World Congress on Evangelism in Berlin in 1966. Then came various regional conferences, including a conference for Asian evangelical leaders in Singapore in 1968, and a European conference on evangelism in 1971. Then we convened another world congress in Lausanne, Switzerland, in 1974. In all these conferences, even though much of the responsibility fell on me and was organized and financed by the Billy Graham Evangelistic Association, I chose to be called the "Honorary Chairman," and appointed Chairmen and Program Directors to be responsible for the day-to-day administration.

These were all memorable and worthwhile meetings which brought together theologians, educators, mission executives, pastors, and church leaders, as well as evangelists. In retrospect, they probably laid an essential foundation for Amsterdam '83. But always in my mind and heart was the original vision of a conference strictly for evangelists. The question was, however, how could we distinguish between the pastor with the gift of an evangelist and one who, like me, travels from place to place preaching the Gospel? That's when we thought the word "itinerant" made the definition more specific.

But, strange as it seems now, when we discussed the possibility of this event, we discovered that initially few people shared the vision. However, as time went on, we were amazed at the enthusiasm which grew as news of the Conference spread.

In those early days we didn't envisage a budget of more than a million dollars — we never dreamed it would reach eight million! We had no idea of how many evangelists would be involved and from where they would all come. But as astronomical as eight million dollars seems, I am convinced that it was worth every dollar so carefully spent. The way the Lord provided the funds is a story in itself! People contributed from all over the world. As the preparations gained momentum, people in various countries prayed and God answered their prayers beyond our greatest expectations.

Where would the Conference be held? Amsterdam was chosen for many reasons. The Dutch are extremely hospitable people, and we knew there would be no visa problems for participants from any part of the world. The magnificent facilities of the RAI make it one of the finest conference centers in the world — one of the few facilities in the world able to accommodate one hundred eighty workshops (with room to spare). Holland's great airline, KLM, promised their cooperation not only with worldwide transportation but in the awesome task of feeding everyone during the entire Conference. They delivered on those promises superbly, feeding five thousand people at one sitting in fewer than fifty minutes.

God gave us some wonderful men to fill positions of leadership. Walter H. Smyth, BGEA's Vice-President in charge of international affairs, became Chairman. The man appointed Director was a longtime friend, colleague, and chairman of our work in Germany, Werner Bürklin. He gathered around him one of the finest teams of dedicated workers I have ever seen anywhere in the world. Leighton Ford was asked to be Program Chairman, and Campus Crusade for Christ loaned us Paul Eshleman to serve as Program Director. I remember an early committee meeting at which Paul outlined his vision, and he expanded my thinking a thousandfold as to the longterm potential of the Conference.

Bob Williams of our staff was asked to come and head up the selection of participants. What a job he had! At first we thought in terms of a few hundred itinerant evangelists, not dreaming there were so many in the world. For several years we collected names of itinerant evangelists — a task which had never been done before. The large number greatly surpassed our expectations. The thousands of applications from qualified men and women far exceeded the number of places available. Some two hundred committees around the world helped the process of selection. We were determined not to miss those comparatively unknown evangelists working faithfully in earth's remotest areas.

I'll never forget the day the Conference opened. It was one of the hottest days ever recorded in Amsterdam! The main auditorium was like a huge oven, as one hundred and fifty blue-jacketed stewards and stewardesses, recruited from Christian colleges and organizations, ushered some four thousand participants (together with a thousand more observers, visitors, press, and others) to their places.

As I viewed the scene from the platform, my heart was filled with gratitude to God. The vision He gave me so many years before was being fulfilled in His perfect timing.

In that opening ceremony there was a parade with the flags of the one hundred and thirty-three nations represented. Here before me were the men and women who are part of God's army of evangelists to complete Jesus' Great Commission. Their faces, with eager smiles and shining eyes, showed the enthusiasm with which they had come. Many of them had never before been outside their own country, some not even outside their own province! Some had just completed their first journey by air. Coming to Amsterdam was a great experience in which everything was new and fresh. We got a new glimpse of the world through their eyes. And their determination to work hard at absorbing all we shared together was evidence enough of the depth of their dedication.

In his book about the Conference, *Billy Graham, A Vision Imparted*, Dave Foster describes the way I closed that opening session:

"By the time he reached the climax of his introductory talk and offered a prayer of dedication and commitment, the Conference was 'catching fire.' There was already a sense of renewal in the hearts of participants, evidenced by the fervent and unrestrained singing of the final hymn with the well-chosen verse . . .

> *My gracious Master and my God,*
> *Assist me to proclaim,*
> *To spread through all the earth abroad*
> *The honors of Thy Name.*

"As Walter Smyth left the platform, . . . he summed up the spirit which was already evident, the oneness, the love, the praise and worship.

" 'This Conference,' he commented, 'seems to be starting at a point where others finish.' "

One person whose massive contribution to the Conference helped make this true is one of my closest friends and colleagues, Cliff Barrows. He took charge of the platform throughout the Conference; in all the years of my ministry I have never found anyone who does this better. And the music program he led at Amsterdam was truly magnificent. Even the well-chosen songs and choruses became unforgettably linked to this great event. I can never hear or sing *"Emmanuel, God with us"* or *"Freely, freely, you have received . . ."* without my thoughts being drawn back to Amsterdam.

But the Conference was more than a great time of fellowship and worship with fellow-evangelists; it was also a period of serious and strategic thinking and praying concerning the completion of the Great Commission. For example, instructional ideas for a syllabus for teaching itinerant evangelism worldwide were brought together. Scores of evangelists expressed interest in this. Dr. Lewis Drummond, Professor of Evangelism at the Southern Baptist Theological Seminary in Louisville, Kentucky, who was given responsibility for this, said, ''I came to Amsterdam expecting to sit down with no more than twenty professors of evangelism to prepare the requested syllabus. I never expected so many evangelists to be so interested in developing a curriculum in itinerant evangelism.'' In this and many other ways Amsterdam '83 was the catalyst for continuing expressions of concern for evangelism, and will continue to be in the future.

In addition, Amsterdam '83 was also a catalyst for active evangelism during the Conference itself. To bring evangelism from a theologically based definition to its practical expression, the evangelists who came to Amsterdam devoted one afternoon to going out into the streets, on to Holland's North Sea beaches, into the city's many parks, and wherever they could make contact with people and share their faith.

I was eager to participate in this Afternoon of Witness, but I had a problem. Whenever the news media publicize my presence in an area, it's hard to walk around unrecognized. So I dressed in old blue jeans, a cap, and dark glasses before going with my colleague, T. W. Wilson, to mingle with the crowds in a park. I handed out tracts on the four steps to peace with God, and I tried to witness. The response was not exactly encouraging. In fact, I got practically nowhere!

Then I saw a small group of Africans from the Ivory Coast. They were witnessing to a young Dutch student. At first he looked as though he wanted to get away, but they were so sweet and gracious that he just couldn't seem to escape! They had their Bibles open and were showing him passages of Scripture. I joined them and sat down to listen. I had never heard a better witness in my life!

In Amsterdam, God enabled us to learn from one another. And one thing I learned from the people we were trying to reach was that they were interested in the Person of Christ more than in religion, or organized Christianity, or the church. It was the Person of Christ who would capture their attention.

When we were trying to determine whom we should invite to Amsterdam, we had to establish guidelines by beginning with the basic question, "What is an evangelist?" While we know that every Christian should be a witness to Christ, we are also aware that God has called certain people into the specific task or ministry of evangelism.

An evangelist is a person with a special gift from the Holy Spirit to announce the good news of the Gospel. Methods may differ according to the evangelist's opportunity and calling, but the central truth remains: an evangelist has been called and especially equipped by God to declare the Gospel to those who have not accepted it, with the goal of challenging them to turn to Christ in repentance and faith.

The Greek word in the New Testament for "evangelist" means "one who announces the good news." In its verb form, meaning "to announce the good news," it occurs more than fifty times. The noun "evangelist," used to designate the one who brought the good news, was apparently rare in the ancient world, although it is used three times in the New Testament. Let's look briefly at each of those three occurrences to understand what the Bible means when it speaks about an evangelist.

The most general reference to the evangelist is found in Ephesians 4:11, where Paul declares that God "gave some to be apostles, some to be prophets, some to be evangelists, and some to be pastors and teachers" (NIV). *This New Testament gift and office of the evangelist has never been withdrawn from the church.* It is not only a legitimate ministry, it is a God-given ministry to be used — like all gifts — "so that the body of Christ may be built up" (Ephesians 4:12, NIV).

It is tragic that at times the church has lost sight of the legitimacy and importance of the ministry of the evangelist. Unfortunately, sometimes the evangelists themselves have added to the problem by their failure to cooperate as fully as possible with churches. However, certainly one of the greatest needs in the world church today is the recovery of belief in the *necessity of evangelism* and the recovery of belief in the *legitimacy and the necessity of the evangelist.* To quote the former Anglican Archbishop of Sidney, Sir Marcus Loane, who gave a major address at Amsterdam: "It may be all too easy to think that the age of evangelism . . . has come to an end. But this is the kind of thinking that leads to the blight which rests on the church whose vision has failed. . . . When vision and outreach fail, the church is left with the problem of nominalism in its own ranks. This in inbred; it is inward-looking; it is lacking in true spiritual vitality."

The other two New Testament references to the evangelist refer to specific men. In Acts 21:8 Philip is called an evangelist; and in Paul's second letter Timothy is charged to "do the work of an evangelist" (2 Timothy 4:5). We took that admonition as the theme of Amsterdam '83.

The work of the evangelist is well illustrated by these

two men. We read of Philip that "he preached the good news of the kingdom of God and the name of Jesus Christ" (Acts 8:12, NIV). In his illuminating analysis of Philip's life and work Dr. Stephen F. Olford, in his address at Amsterdam, pointed out three characteristics of Philip — characteristics that should be true of every evangelist. First, *Philip was a worker* in the church, and evangelism must always have its roots as much as possible in the church. Then, *Philip was also a preacher* in the world, going from place to place to those who did not know the Gospel or had not turned to Christ. Finally, *Philip did not neglect* his own family responsibilities; in fact, he had four daughters who were known for their spiritual gifts and work. In similar fashion Paul could write of Timothy that he "is our brother and God's fellow worker in spreading the gospel of Christ" (1 Thessalonians 3:2, NIV).

That is what evangelism is all about — "spreading the gospel of Christ." It is more than a *method*, however; it is also a *message*. It is the message of God's love; of man's sin; of Christ's death, burial, and resurrection; and of God's forgiveness. It is a message that demands a response — a response of faith, followed by discipleship. The term "evangelism" encompasses every effort to declare the good news of Jesus Christ to the end that people may understand God's offer of salvation and respond in faith and discipleship.

As The Lausanne Covenant defines it: "To evangelize is to spread the good news that Jesus Christ died for our sins and was raised from the dead according to the Scriptures, and that as the reigning Lord He now offers forgiveness of sins and the liberating gift of the Holy Spirit to all who repent and believe. ... Evangelism itself is the proclamation of the historical, biblical Christ as Savior and Lord, with a view to persuading people to come to Him personally and so be reconciled to God. In issuing the gospel invitation we have no liberty to conceal the cost of discipleship. ... The results of evangelism include obedience to Christ, incorporation into His

Church and responsible service in the world."[1]

The zeal and the dedication to evangelism which characterized the Christians of the first century should mark the life of the church today. The task has not changed. The spiritual needs of humanity have not changed. The good news of the Gospel has not changed. And God's gifts to the church — including the gift of the evangelist — have not changed. Amsterdam '83 meant many different things to all those who attended. For some participants the greatest impact of Amsterdam '83 may have been its affirmation of the role of the evangelist. For others it may have been a solemn time of rededication to the task of evangelism. But whatever it meant to each individual who participated, I doubt if anyone went away unchanged as we grasped the greatness of our task and the power of God to accomplish His purposes.

For identification and security reasons all who attended the Conference were required to be fitted with a plastic wristband. This was worn day and night throughout our time together. It could not be removed without actually cutting it off, and participants were requested not to do this until leaving Amsterdam. But, interestingly enough, this simple plastic band became more than a means of identification for some of the evangelists. Many kept it on their wrists long after the Conference finished as a reminder of commitments they had made before the Lord in Amsterdam, especially as they declared the Affirmations about which this commentary is written. Some of those wristbands are still being worn today, in Africa, Asia, South America, and other parts of the world!

As preparations were made for Amsterdam '83, many people from various parts of the world asked if there would be some type of final statement that the Conference would issue, just as the Lausanne Covenant had come from the 1974 Lausanne Congress on World Evangelization. After careful deliberation it was decided that Amsterdam '83 would not issue a final statement that attempted to summarize the results of the Conference, especially since its focus would be on practical matters concerning evangelism. At the same time many evangelists from widely different backgrounds expressed the hope that some type of brief ''code of standards'' for evangelists could be prepared. To make a long story short, a carefully selected international committee under the chairmanship of Dr. Kenneth Kantzer was appointed to prepare this. They worked intensely during the Conference. Their preliminary draft was presented to a representative group of evangelists from various parts of the world, who gave the committee many valuable suggestions. Their final draft — The Amsterdam Affirmations — stated briefly but thoroughly the biblical foundation, the task, and the integrity of the evangelist. At the closing service the participants of the Conference joined in affirming verbally their commitment to each of the fifteen affirmations.

It was suggested that I write an interpretative commentary on the Amsterdam Affirmations, which I agreed to do. To help me do this I called on my friends and colleagues John Akers, Art Johnston, Dave Foster, and Stephen F. Olford. Through the years I have often depended on my Team members and friends to help me in the preparation of sermons, articles, and books, and I am deeply grateful for the willingness of those who have assisted and advised me in this project.

It is my prayer that God will use this commentary on The Amsterdam Affirmations to help not only itinerant evangelists, but to help many other Christians as well to gain a greater vision for God's work in our world. God has placed us in a unique and opportune period of history. The fields are ''ripe for harvest.'' And while ''some have special ability in winning people to Christ'' (Ephesians 4:11, TLB), all God's people are to be His witnesses. May this commentary therefore circulate far beyond that group who stood at Amsterdam '83 and committed themselves to these Affirmations, and may we see a renewed dedication in this generation to the priority of evangelism on the part of every child of God.

Affirmation I

I read publicly the following Affirmation:

We confess Jesus Christ as God,
our Lord and Savior, who is revealed in the Bible, which is the
infallible Word of God.

*More than four thousand itinerant evangelists
replied audibly:*

I affirm.

Why is Christianity so different from every other
religion in the world? What makes the message of the
evangelist unique? What is distinctive about Christian
discipleship?

The answer to all these questions focuses not on
the practice of religion, nor primarily on a plan for
living, but on the Person of Jesus Christ. Jesus, Son of
God the Father and Second Person of the Trinity, is
the central figure of our evangelistic message.

Today many voices are making other claims. Athe-
ists say there is no God. Polytheism may allow that
Jesus is one of many gods. When I went to some Far
Eastern countries, I had to learn that in giving the
invitation I needed to make it clear to my listeners that
they were turning *from* all other gods and turning *to* the
true and the living God as revealed in the Scriptures.
Many evangelists from America or Europe can go to

some of those countries and get thousands of people to respond to their appeals, but what they are doing is just making Jesus one of many gods that they worship. Some say Jesus is the first of the divine creation, but not eternally God. But we, as "ambassadors for Christ" (see 2 Corinthians 5:20), boldly echo the ringing conviction of the apostle Peter when he affirmed, "Thou art the Christ, the Son of the living God" (Matthew 16:16). The title "Christ" means "anointed one." It is the term, in the Greek language, for the ancient Hebrew word "Messiah" — the "anointed one" whom God would send to save His people. Peter and his fellow Jews, the first believers of the early Christian church, recognized Jesus as the Messiah promised in the Old Testament. Their period and part of world history was one of discouragement and despair. The promised Messiah shone as a beacon in the darkness, and His light has never dimmed. "In him was life; and the life was the light of men. . . . the true Light, which lighteth every man that cometh into the world" (John 1:4,9).

Today, as world leaders struggle with seemingly insurmountable problems, as storm clouds gather around the globe, this darkening and menacing situation simply accentuates the brightness of the One who proclaimed, "I am the light of the world: he that followeth me shall not walk in darkness, but shall have the light of life" (John 8:12). He is "the Lamb of God, which taketh away the sin of the world" (John 1:29). He is the promised Messiah of ancient Israel. He is the hope of the hopeless, helpless Gentiles — which includes most of the population of the world, whether they be African, Asian, American, or European.

In all my evangelistic ministry I have never felt a need to "adapt" Jesus to the many and varied nationalities, cultures, tribes, or ethnic groups to whom I have preached. I believe in contextualization. That is that we adapt our methods and terminology to the people to whom we are ministering. I try to adapt illustrations or emphasize certain truths that will help a particular audience understand the Gospel more clearly in light of their cultural background. But the essential truths of the Gospel do not change. All things were created by Him and He sustains all creation, so the message of His saving grace is applicable to all. The facts concerning His virgin birth, His sinless life, His sacrificial and substitutionary death, His resurrection and ascension to the right hand of the Father, and the glorious hope of His return must not be diluted or distorted in any way.

Jesus is not only the Christ, He is also "God, our Lord and Savior." This is a staggering, almost incomprehensible truth: God Himself has come down on this planet in the person of His only Son. The incarnation and the full deity of Jesus are the cornerstones of the Christian faith. Jesus Christ was not just a great teacher or a holy religious leader. He was God Himself in human flesh — fully God and fully man.

This great truth is underlined throughout the New Testament. John begins his Gospel, "In the beginning was the Word. . . ." (Here we have the perfect example of contextualization, used by the apostle John in writing for the Greek mind. He did not take the Christian concept of Jesus as the "Word" from Jewish messianic ideas or Jewish ways of thinking. The word "logos" in Greek, translated "word," was understood by both Hebrew and Greek minds.) Then John continues, "And the Word was with God, and the Word was God. . . . And the Word was made flesh, and dwelt among us, (and we beheld his glory, the glory as of the only begotten of the Father,) full of grace and truth" (John 1:1,14). Christ is from eternity to eternity, because He is fully God. The Bible says, "He is the image of the invisible God, the firstborn over all creation. For by him all things were created. . . . For God was pleased to have all his fullness dwell in him" (Colossians 1:15–16,19, NIV). Matthew tells us of the birth of Jesus and states, "All this was done, that it might be fulfilled which was spoken of the Lord by the prophet, saying, Behold, a virgin shall be with child, and shall bring forth a son, and they shall call his name Emmanuel, which being interpreted is, God with us" (Matthew 1:22–23).

Jesus Himself gave frequent witness to His uniqueness and His divine nature. To His opponents He declared, "Before Abraham was, I am" (John 8:58). They immediately recognized this as a clear claim to divinity and tried to stone Him for blasphemy. On another occasion Jesus stated, "I and my Father are one" (John 10:30) — and again His enemies tried to stone Him "because that thou, being a man, makest thyself God" (John 10:33). Furthermore, He demonstrated the power to do things that only God can do, such as forgive sins (Mark 2:1–12). The charge brought against Him at His trial was that "He made himself the Son of God" (John 19:7); and when asked if He was the Son of God, He replied, "You are right in saying I am" (Luke 22:70, NIV).

Was Jesus deluded in making that claim? Or is it true? What proof did He offer that He was truly God come in human form?

First, there was the proof of *His perfect life*. He could ask, "Which of you convinceth me of sin?" (John 8:46) — and no one could answer, because His life was perfect. Those who schemed to bring Him to trial had to obtain false witnesses to bring charges, because He was blameless. He was able to confront the full fury of Satan's temptations and yet not yield to sin; He "was in all points tempted like as we are, yet without sin" (Hebrews 4:15; see John 8:46; 2 Corinthians 5:21; 1 Peter 1:19).

Second, there was the evidence of *His power*. His power was the power of God almighty — the power only God has. He had power over the forces of nature; He could quiet the storms on the sea of Galilee (see Matthew 8:23–27; Mark 4:35–41; Luke 8:22–25). He had power over sickness and disease; He raised the dead, healed the sick, restored sight to the blind, and made the lame walk (see Matthew 8:1-3; Mark 1:40-2:12; Luke 7:12-15). His miracles were a witness to the fact that He is Lord of all nature. "For by him were all things created. . . . And he is before all things, and by him all things consist" (Colossians 1:16-17).

Third, there was the evidence of *fulfilled prophecy.* Hundreds of years before his birth the prophets of the Old Testament spoke precisely of the place where He would be born (Micah 5:2), and the manner of His death and burial (Psalm 22; Isaiah 53). Uncounted details of His life were foretold by the prophets, and in every instance these prophecies were fulfilled. That is why Jesus could say to the bewildered disciples on the road to Emmaus, "O fools, and slow of heart to believe all that the prophets have spoken: Ought not Christ to have suffered these things, and to enter into his glory? And beginning at Moses and all the prophets, he expounded unto them in all the scriptures the things concerning himself" (Luke 24:25-27).

Fourth, there was the evidence of *His resurrection from the dead.* Jesus Christ was "declared to be the Son of God with power, according to the spirit of holiness, by the resurrection from the dead" (Romans 1:4). The founders of the various non-Christian religions of the world have lived, died, and been buried; in some instances it is still possible to visit their graves. But Christ is alive! His resurrection is a fact! His tomb is empty — and this is a compelling and central proof of His unique divine nature as God in human flesh (see 1 Corinthians 15).

Fifth, there is the proof of *changed lives.* History vividly illustrates what the Bible clearly affirms, "The heart is deceitful above all things, and desperately wicked: who can know it?" (Jeremiah 17:9). Education and discipline can do no more than rub off the rough edges of human selfishness — but Christ alone, the divine Son of God, has power to change the human heart. And He does (see 1 Timothy 1:12-16). Christ can take the most sin-laden, selfish, evil person and bring forgiveness and new life. The Bible says, "If any man be in Christ, he is a new creature: old things are passed away; behold, all things are become new" (2 Corinthians 5:17). His power to change the human heart is a further proof of His divine nature (see Luke 5:17,24–26).

Yes, Jesus Christ is who He said He is: God Himself in human form. And that is a crucial truth which undergirds the reality of our salvation. Only a divine Savior could truly die as the perfect and complete sacrifice for our sins. Only a divine Lord could tell us how we should live. Only the risen and ascended Son of God is worthy of our worship and our service. *"We confess Jesus Christ as God, our Lord and Savior."*

During His time here on earth, He was God in the flesh, true God and true man. He is from eternity to eternity. Jesus Christ, by His death and resurrection, *became* the Gospel. As His ambassadors we must represent Him in all His fullness totally and truthfully. Anything less disqualifies us from our high and holy calling.

The Nicene Creed that came out of the Council of Nicaea in A.D. 325 affirmed He is "very God of very God, . . . being of one substance with the Father."

By faith Jesus becomes *our* Lord and Savior. All authority in heaven and on earth has been given to Him (Matthew 28:18). The present evil world system does not yet acknowledge His Lordship; it is still under the deceiving power of the prince of this world, Satan (Ephesians 2:2). But those whom Jesus indwells have authority over the evil one and all his demons. The apostle John declares, "Greater is he that is in you, than he that is in the world" (1 John 4:4).

Therefore, in spite of our human limitations and even our failures as evangelists, the Lord is sovereignly directing His own work of redemption through our evangelism. And we are linked to the vast resources of His power so that we don't merely "get by" in our lives and ministries, but "in all these things we are *more than conquerors through him*" (Romans 8:37). And as the context of that inspiring and reassuring verse promises, nothing will "be able to separate us from the love of God, which is in Christ Jesus our Lord" (Romans 8:39). God can turn the greatest of tragedies into that which is for our good and for His glory, for "we know that all things work together for good to them that love God, to them who are the called according to his purpose" (Romans 8:28).

Because Jesus is Savior, He saves us from the *penalty* of sin (see Matthew 1:21). Because He is Lord, He, by His Holy Spirit, gives us *power* over sin as we daily walk with Him (see Hebrews 7:25). And some future day He will take us to be with Himself, far from the very *presence* of sin (see Hebrews 9:28). Only because Jesus is God and we have confessed Him as Savior and Lord, can He bestow and we receive these benefits, this blessed assurance and hope (see Romans 10:9).

How do we have assurance? How do we know these things are true? In many ways, but primarily because, as our Affirmation states, they are "revealed in the Bible, which is the infallible Word of God."

How can we know the truth about God? Must we grope around in the dark, only guessing and never knowing the truth? Is religion just a matter of personal opinion or viewpoint, with one philosopher's ideas as good as the next? The Bible says "no"! It tells us that we *can* know the truth — because God has revealed Himself to us.

Since man's fall in the Garden of Eden (Genesis 3), God has continued to reveal Himself in history (Hebrews 1:1-3). God chose a man, Abraham (Genesis 12:1-3), who became a great nation, the Hebrews. He miraculously delivered His chosen people from Egypt. Under Moses' leadership they crossed the Red Sea (Exodus 14). He gave them the Ten Commandments (Exodus 20; Deuteronomy 6; Romans 9:4). He gave Israel prophets whose divinely inspired predictions were absolutely trustworthy (Deuteronomy 13:1–5; 18:20–22). Unfortunately, the Hebrews constantly complained, disobeyed, and even defied God. At times they turned to other gods. God brought judgment after judgment on them for their disobedience. Thus the history of the Jewish people, though chosen of God, is one of revival, blessing, and judgment.

But most of all, He revealed Himself in the Person of His Son, Jesus Christ. "No man hath seen God at any time; the only begotten Son, which is in the bosom of the Father, he hath declared him" (John 1:18). He confirmed that Jesus is truly God the Son by His miracles, and by raising Him from the dead (Luke 24:44–48; Acts 2:32). The message and faith of the evangelist are anchored in what God has done in history. They are not anchored in a church, religious traditions, or personal feelings. They are anchored in the assurance of what God has done in history, recorded, and revealed in the Bible.

If the evangelist is to "preach the Word" (2 Timothy 4:2) with authority and power, he must be firmly convinced of two things.

First, he must be convinced that the Bible, the written Word of God, was prepared under the direction of the Holy Spirit, who preserved the authors from departing from God's revelation in their writing so that they conveyed exactly what God wanted them to record. "Knowing this first, that no prophecy of the scripture is of any private interpretation. For the prophecy came not in old time by the will of man: but holy men of God spake as they were moved by the Holy Ghost" (2 Peter 1:20–21). Even though the human writers of Scripture wrote as sons of their time and their own personalities often shine through in their writings, God ensured that the words and thoughts were inspired and recorded accurately as He intended. "All scripture is given by inspiration of God, and is profitable for doctrine, for reproof, for correction, for instruction in righteousness: That the man of God may be perfect, throughly furnished unto all good works" (2 Timothy 3:16-17).

Because it is God's inspired Word, the Bible does not contradict itself or teach falsehoods — because God cannot lie. With our human limitations we may not always understand every detail of Scripture, but we must never lose sight of the fact that it is God's Word and not man's ideas or opinions. As The Lausanne Covenant declares, "We affirm the divine inspiration, truthfulness, and authority of both the Old and New Testament Scriptures in their entirety as the only written word of God, without error in all that it affirms, and the only infallible rule of faith and practice."[1] Jesus constantly quoted the Old Testament and made it clear that it was the inspired Word of God. We who follow Christ must have just as high a view of Scripture as He did (see John 10:34; Matthew 5:17).

Second, if the evangelist is to preach with authority and power, he must be convinced that the Word of God has the power to change lives (1 Corinthians 2:1-5). God has not promised to bless our eloquence or our human energy — but He has promised to bless His Word. "For as the rain cometh down, and the snow from heaven, and returneth not thither, but watereth the earth, and maketh it bring forth and bud, that it may give seed to the sower, and bread to the eater: So shall my word be that goeth forth out of my mouth: it shall not return unto me void, but it shall accomplish that which I please, and it shall prosper in the thing whereto I sent it" (Isaiah 55:10-11).

Time after time in my ministry I have quoted a Bible verse in a sermon — sometimes without planning to do so in advance — and had someone tell me afterward that it was that verse which the Holy Spirit used to bring conviction or faith to him. "Is not my word like as a fire? saith the Lord; and like a hammer that breaketh the rock in pieces?" (Jeremiah 23:29). Don't let anything or anyone shake your confidence in the trustworthiness, authority, and power of the Bible.

Make it your guide for your life and your ministry, no matter what the future may hold for you.

At one time in my life I had a struggle believing the Bible to be the authoritative Word of God. Some professors and other intellectuals were expressing their own doubts about it and pointing to alleged contradictions in the Bible. I was young, just out of school, and was having my first experiences in preaching. Seeds of doubt began to grow and I struggled over this question of the integrity of the Word of God. Then one moonlit night in the mountains of California I went out alone with my Bible. The turmoil in my mind was a sharp contrast to the peace and serenity of the natural beauty around me. Finally, I laid my open Bible on the stump of a tree and prayed, ''Oh, Lord, I don't understand everything in this Book, but I accept it by faith as the Word of the living God.'' And I can truly say that since that moment I've never doubted that the Bible is the Word of God. Furthermore, God has confirmed this to me time after time, as I have witnessed the power of the Word of God at work in the lives of people.

Since that time I have discovered that we need not fear the allegations or arguments of those who would deny the Bible's authority. There is external and internal evidence to show the absolute trustworthiness of the Bible. Externally, there is the evidence from such fields as archaeology and linguistics. Internally, there is the final word of the Lord Jesus Himself, who authenticated the Old Testament (see John 10:34; Matthew 5:17) and anticipated the New Testament (John 16:13–14). He employed and expounded the Old Testament as an infallible authority (see Luke 24:27,44). We cannot examine the history, unity, and prophecy of God's Word — let alone its saying and sanctifying power in our own lives as evangelists — without believing in its divine inspiration and authority.

The evangelist must be thoroughly convinced of the infallibility of Scripture. Only then can he preach with authority God's *promise* of salvation and forgiveness to all who call on the name of the Lord, and God's *warning* of judgment for those who do not.

We respect God-guided decisions of church councils. We praise Him for leadership He has raised up in His church throughout the ages. We are grateful for the heritage of church traditions which are in accordance with biblical teaching. But our authority as evangelists does not originate in any of these. Our call and power to evangelize comes from the pages of this infallible Word of God — the Bible.

This collection of sixty-six books, written over a period of many centuries yet forming a complete and accurate divine revelation, has been carefully handed down to us from the apostles of our Lord. Some is the very Scripture that Jesus Himself read and taught while here on earth. In it He is revealed. Him we believe, Him we trust, Him we proclaim as Savior, and Him we confess before others as our Lord. He is the same yesterday, today, and forever (Hebrews 13:8).

Because Jesus is one with God and was sent by the Father into human history (John 20:21), the cross is an objective demonstration of divine love (Romans 5:8). Our faith is built on the fact of Christ's resurrection.

That is why we rejoice! That is the foundation of the truth we declare and the kingdom we extend as we ''do the work of an evangelist.''

Affirmation II

⟨✿⟩

I read aloud the second Affirmation:

We affirm our commitment to the Great Commission of our Lord, and we declare our willingness to go anywhere, do anything, and sacrifice anything God requires of us in the fulfillment of that Commission.

Four thousand, in unison,
almost shouted back:

I affirm.

⟨✿⟩

It is hard to imagine what must have been passing through the minds of that little band of eleven disciples as they clustered around the risen Lord Jesus Christ on a mountain somewhere in Galilee. They recently had gone through the misery of apparent defeat, watching helplessly as Jesus was nailed to a cross. Their dreams of a world kingdom under Christ's rule were shattered. Then came the reports from the women who had visited the tomb early on that first Easter morning — reports that He was alive! At first they doubted; but as time went on, they knew the reports to be true, for Jesus Himself appeared to them many times. Finally, He comes to them and issues the greatest challenge they — or we — could ever hear: "All power is given unto me in heaven and in earth. Go ye therefore, and teach all nations, baptizing them in the name of the Father, and of the Son, and of the Holy Ghost: Teaching them to observe all things whatsoever I have commanded you: and, lo, I am with you alway, even unto the end of the world" (Matthew 28:18-20).

These words of commission need to be restudied and obeyed by the whole church, and especially by those of us who are evangelists. In that one statement the Master summarized all that we require for our task.

Jesus commanded — GO WITH MY POWER. "All power [authority] is given unto me in heaven and in earth. Go ... " (Matthew 28:18-19). Without that announcement of His authority, the Great Commission would have lacked justification and motivation. But under that authority, we can direct divine power from heaven and destroy demonic power on earth. Jesus has *all* power in heaven and on earth! As John Stott put it (at the World Congress on Evangelism in Berlin in 1966), "The authority of Jesus Christ extends over all creatures, whether human or superhuman, over the church, over nations, over the devil and his works."

Jesus commanded — GO WITH MY PROGRAM. "Go ... make disciples of all the nations, baptizing them in the name of the Father and of the Son and of the Holy Spirit, teaching them to observe all things whatever I have commanded you" (Matthew 28:19-20, NKJV). We are to *evangelize* men and women. The New English Bible renders this, "Make all nations my disciples" (Matthew 28:19, NEB). That personal pronoun makes it clear that our task is not only to call for decisions for Christ, but to make disciples for Christ. Also, we are to *baptize* men and women. We are to bring converts into the fellowship of the church. This is the significance of the ONE name of the Father,

Son, and Holy Spirit. We are to *catechize* men and women. We are to "[warn] every man, and [teach] every man in all wisdom; that we may present every man perfect in Christ Jesus" (Colossians 1:28).

Jesus commanded — GO WITH MY PRESENCE. "Lo, I am with you alway, even unto the end of the world" (Matthew 28:20). In the person of the Holy Spirit, Jesus has promised to be with us every day, and come what may — until the task is finished — and to the end of time. What a promise, what a comfort!

No doubt the disciples were startled by this Great Commission. Eleven men going into all the world, making disciples from all nations? In the Acts of the Apostles we read that the apostle James, in his address, outlined God's plan for the future to call out "a people for his name" (Acts 15:14). Many times Christian workers become discouraged because they don't see more results, or they don't see a great turning to God or great revivals that they had hoped to see or that they had read about in history. However, God is still at work calling out a people from all kindreds and tribes for His Name. We know from Scripture that the whole world is not going to turn to Christ voluntarily (see Romans 10:13–21).

When I go to a city to hold an evangelistic Crusade, I do not expect the whole city to turn to Christ; I have never been to a town or a village anywhere in the world where I thought the majority of the people to be true believers. But I do know that within that city God has "much people" ("I have much people in this city," Acts 18:10). I also believe when I go to a city that there are people whose hearts God has prepared already for the message and they will respond to receive Christ as their Lord and Savior (see Acts 10:1–48; 16:14–15). In some instances, there may be many (as at Pentecost), or there may be few (as the apostle Paul experienced in Athens after his sermon at Mars Hill, see Acts 17:32–34). The task was humanly impossible — but with God all things are possible! They were to do their part, and within a generation that little band had grown until groups of Christians were to be found throughout much of the Roman Empire. They were changed from a dispirited, bewildered group of men to a fearless team of evangelists who were willing to *go* anywhere, *do* anything, and *sacrifice* anything "for the sake of the Gospel." No wonder the early Christians were called by their enemies men who had "turned the world upside down" (Acts 17:6). They were the first men and women who set the pace for the generations to follow. Like runners carrying the Olympic flame, they would continue to relay the message of Christ down through the centuries until our own time.

The Great Commission is still in effect. Christ's command has not changed, and neither has God's great plan of redemption. God's method of reaching the world with the message of Christ is still the same. "It pleased God by the foolishness of preaching to save them that believe" (1 Corinthians 1:21). The call of God to His people is to proclaim the Gospel to the ends of the earth. "How then shall they call on him in whom they have not believed? and how shall they believe in him of whom they have not heard? and how shall they hear without a preacher? And how shall they preach, except they be sent?" (Romans 10:14–15). The proclamation of the Gospel — by whatever means, and wherever God places us — is the great responsibility and privilege of His people. "But ye are a chosen generation, a royal priesthood, an holy nation, a peculiar people; that ye should shew forth the praises of him who hath called you out of darkness into his marvelous light" (1 Peter 2:9).

Jesus had two important verbs in His vocabulary. One was *come* and the other was *go*.

This command, we must never forget, is from the Lord Himself. It is not a program thought up by a committee or a scheme planned by a group of enthusiastic people. Even if we had no other reason to go and proclaim the Gospel, the command of Christ would be enough. "All authority" has been given to Him. Dare we disobey the command of God Himself? Dare we place personal comfort or security before the sovereign call of God?

Let us also never forget that this command has been given to *all* God's people. Paul thanked God for the Roman Christians because "your faith is spoken of throughout the whole world" (Romans 1:8). Of the Thessalonian Christians Paul said, "From you sounded out the word of the Lord not only in Macedonia and Achaia, but also in every place your faith to God-ward is spread abroad" (1 Thessalonians 1:8). When persecution broke out against the early church, the apostles stayed in Jerusalem, but the rest of the Christians "went every where preaching the word" (Acts 8:4).

I have discovered that one of the most important longterm effects of our evangelistic crusades wherever we go is the mobilization of large numbers of believers in a community to do personal witnessing — often for the first time. In all of our crusades, months before the meetings begin, we have the Christian Life and Witness Classes where we train hundreds, and even thousands, of Christians to witness by their lives and by their words. We teach them how to lead others to Christ. They are the ones who become counselors in our crusades. Then within the churches we have Nurture Groups that are able to nurture these new believers when they come into the church. So we try to train both the individual believers and the churches themselves, including the pastors. All Christians — to the end of the age — are to be involved in bringing the good news of the Gospel to those who do not know Christ.

As we have seen, God has also entrusted the special gift of evangelism to some specially skilled in communication who are to give leadership in carrying on this central mission of the church. As evangelists we are united not only in a common confession, but in a common commitment to the Great Commission.

Twentieth-century evangelists live in a period without parallel in human history. For the first time man has the awesome ability to obliterate human life on this planet. Man's sinfulness has the world on a course toward self-destruction. The Great Commission becomes an even greater responsibility in the face of such massive moral issues.

We, as God's ambassadors, are called to sound the warning, to make judgment clear, to call sinners to repentance, to announce God's grace, to direct them to Calvary and the God-man on the cross, to point to the empty tomb, to shout the good news from the housetops, to show the way to peace with God and peace between men and nations.

The very nature of God reminds us of His loving desire to redeem and bless all of fallen humanity. He is "longsuffering to us-ward, not willing that any should perish, but that all should come to repentance" (2 Peter 3:9). But while His missionary nature is implied in the Old Testament (Genesis 12:2–3; 2 Chronicles 6:32–33; Isaiah 66:18–23), the New Testament's Great Commission is *explicit*. Time and again we are commanded to evangelize.

But sometimes we, as soldiers of Christ in the forefront of the battle, can succumb to weariness. Perhaps we are less grateful than we should be for our own forgiveness and salvation. Our love for Christ grows cold. Preoccupation with the things of this life dim our evangelistic call. It is then that our Lord's final words, before His ascension to the Father, remind us of the centrality of our commission.

The gift of an evangelist must not be neglected. Failure to use it is disobedience. It can dry up, and our joy in the Lord quickly vanishes. Or we can become "professional." My main motivation as an evangelist is obedience to a divine command and recognition of a God-given gift. But I am also prompted to be faithful to my calling as sometimes I see the sad spectacle of men who were once soul-winners; but then, for one reason or another, were diverted from their prime ministry. No wonder Charles Wesley wrote:

> Happy if with my latest breath
> I may but gasp His name;
> Preach Him to all, and cry in death,
> "Behold, behold the lamb."

I am aware that fulfillment of our Commission will vary with each evangelist. Some, because of failing health, intense persecution, and even martyrdom, may finish their task early in life. Such was the case with Jesus Himself who, at an early age, completed the work God gave Him to do (John 17:4). To others is given a long ministry undergirded by health of body and strength of mind. We dare not retire or seek another ministry without the evident leading of the spirit as sons and servants of God (Romans 8:14). The apostle Paul "fought a good fight, . . . finished [his] course, . . . kept the faith" and was assured of "a crown of righteousness, which the Lord, the righteous judge, shall give" (2 Timothy 4:7-8).

Sacrifice, of one kind or another, will be the constant companion of the itinerant evangelist. Fatigue from travel, loneliness and separation from loved ones, frustration with fellow workers, unsatisfactory living conditions, and disappointing results may take their toll. We may be called to forgo certain pleasures that we see other Christians enjoying.

Many times I have left home to hold an evangelistic crusade; and while I drove from my mountain home, tears have streamed down my face. I did not want my wife or children to realize how I hated to leave — even though I felt an anticipation of the next crusade. I cannot describe the loneliness that I have felt on hundreds, and even thousands, of occasions — in spite of my loyal and wonderful Team and the making of new friends in city after city. Yet nothing could take the place of home. Sometimes I would ask the Lord why He didn't call me to be a pastor or a teacher, so I could stay in one place. There came times when I was almost allergic to another bus station, train station, or in later years an airport! When the planes came, I found that it did not become easier. My schedule just became busier as I adapted it to accommodate airplane travel instead of bus or train travel.

At times it may be hard to see other servants of our same Lord entrusted with greater financial resources. But if we are sure it is *God* who requires this of us — not someone else or even our own imagined sacrifices — it will be easier to take up our cross daily and follow Jesus (Luke 9:23). He knew what it was to be weary, to have poor accommodations, to be misunderstood and mocked. The Bible says He ''was in all points tempted like as we are'' (Hebrews 4:15). The apostle Paul could identify with the sacrifices and discouragements of an evangelistic ministry (2 Corinthians 8:9; 11:16–33). But Paul was encouraged, as we can be, with Jesus' promise that ''whosoever will lose his life for my sake, the same shall save it'' (Luke 9:24).

Endurance, perseverance, and dedication in fulfilling the task of an evangelist result in the most wonderful of all rewards. Nothing in this world can be more thrilling than to hear the Lord of the harvest saying, ''Well done, thou good and faithful servant'' (Matthew 25:21).

I will never forget the powerful sermon delivered in Amsterdam, by Dr. Ed Hill, of the Mt. Zion Missionary Baptist Church in Los Angeles. Throughout his message he urged the evangelists again and again, ''Preach Christ.'' Then he closed by exclaiming to the thrilled and charged delegates — ''He's preachable!''

Affirmation III

---⟨♦⟩---

I read aloud the following Affirmation:

We respond to God's call to the biblical ministry of the evangelist, and accept our solemn responsibility to preach the Word to all peoples as God gives opportunity.

To which the response was:

I affirm.

---⟨♦⟩---

We must be clear about the nature and necessity for evangelism as it is presented to us in the Bible. We must be clear also on the legitimacy and importance of the call to be an evangelist.

How important is evangelism to the church? If a fire is raging in the world, how important is a fire truck? There would be no church without evangelism.

The gift of the evangelist is one of the major spiritual gifts God has given the church (Ephesians 4:11). The gift of the evangelist is just as valid and crucial for the church today as it was in New Testament times.

Paul in his last letter commanded the young pastor Timothy, "Preach the word; ... do the work of an evangelist" (2 Timothy 4:2,5). Tragically the church has often lost sight of the legitimacy and importance of the biblical evangelist. When it has, the church has grown stale and lifeless, shrinking in numbers and spiritual impact. But when it has rediscovered and encouraged the gift of the evangelist, God has blessed the church with spiritual harvests. May God grant that the gift of the evangelist will be seen once again as central in the world church, so that God's people may reach out more effectively to a world that, apart from God, is lost and dying.

God's call to the special ministry of evangelism is distinct from other callings in the ministry of the church. In Acts 21:8 we read that Philip is identified as "the evangelist." Now, this does not detract from the truth that all Christians are called to be witnesses to their Lord and Savior. And pastors, in addition to their shepherding, teaching, and administrative responsibilities, are to be involved in evangelism.

But he who is called *to* and set apart *for* the work of an evangelist is to devote his time and effort singlemindedly to this God-given task. He is not to be distracted by anything likely to deflect him from this. Persecution will not weaken his resolution. The persuasion of others will fall on deaf ears. Only the clear leading of God will cause him to change his ministry.

Often I have been confronted with other legitimate roles in God's Kingdom, but I know they are not for me. For example, I had a wealthy American offer me a thousand acres of land in Florida on the Atlantic Ocean, with millions of dollars to back it up, if I would build a university.

Years earlier the burden had come upon my heart for a graduate university that would compete with Harvard and Yale. I remember riding across Germany and sharing my vision with Dr. Carl F. H. Henry, and I found that he too had had a similar burden. This seemed to be a golden opportunity.

It took me nearly six months to make the decision. The man's father had been an evangelist under whose ministry I had rededicated my life to Christ at a prayer conference in Birmingham, Alabama. On several occasions I went to see the land he offered. I said, ''You have built an empire. What are you going to do with all this money?''

He replied, ''That's why I want you to build a university.''

There we had the property and the money that could eventually lead to one of the biggest endowments in the United States. What was I to do? I conferred with only a handful of my praying friends, and I talked about it a number of times with my wife and my father-in-law, Dr. Nelson Bell. Eventually the decision was made. It would be a diversion of my ministry from evangelism. I knew that God had called me essentially and basically to be an evangelist. When I declined the offer, the man was upset and from that moment on was cool toward me! He felt I had made a tragic mistake. I doubt if he had ever had anyone turn him down before.

The last time I saw him was when Her Majesty the Queen came to the United States in 1976, and President and Mrs. Gerald Ford gave the Queen a State Dinner at the White House. My wife and I were among those invited, as was the man who had offered to give me the land. While we were standing in line to be greeted by the Queen and Prince Philip and President and Mrs. Ford, the man came up to me and said, ''Billy, by this time we could have had a great university if you'd only said yes.''

I replied, ''I feel I did the Lord's will. I'm more sure of it today than ever before. God called me to be an evangelist and I'll never be anything else.''

I have had a number of related opportunities to become involved in television, motion pictures, or Christian education at other institutions. But always the still, small voice has said, ''God called you to be an evangelist.'' And I keep remembering that the apostle Paul insisted, ''This one thing I do.''

An evangelistic gift is to be used, not neglected.

The apostle Paul was "not disobedient unto the heavenly vision" (Acts 26:19). He proclaimed the Gospel. When God calls us, we are to remain faithful.

The apostle Paul both admonished and encouraged his son in the faith, Timothy, about his spiritual gift. He gave him a "don't" and a "do." He said, "Don't minimize your gift." "Do not neglect the gift that is in you" (1 Timothy 4:14, NKJV). The verb here means "not to care." In the parable of the marriage feast we read that those who were invited to the wedding "made light of it" (Matthew 22:5, NKJV). That is our word. We must never minimize our evangelistic gift. God's gifts, like the talent, must never be left unused. Then the apostle urged Timothy, saying, "Do exercise your gift." "Stir up the gift of God which is in you" (2 Timothy 1:6, NKJV). Here the verb means either "to kindle afresh" or "to keep in a full flame." Some of us let the fire burn so low that we lose the incentive to exercise this precious evangelistic gift. We must constantly bear in mind both the "don't" and the "do" of evangelism. Remember the apostle exhorted Timothy to "do the work of an evangelist" (2 Timothy 4:5).

This raises the question, "How do I know if God has called me to be an evangelist?"

The answer to that, most simply stated, is that there is inward certainty from the Holy Spirit and outward confirmation of fellow Christians who walk with God.

The apostle Paul may be considered as a biblical model of an itinerant evangelist. First, Paul was called and appointed by the resurrected Lord (Acts 9:1-9; 26:12-18). Our experience may be quite different to that of Paul. It may be less dramatic, more quiet. But the inward conviction of God's call will be equally certain.

Second, God reveals His will for our lives not only to us but to others who are in fellowship with Him. In Paul's case it was Ananias (Acts 9:10-17). One of the great confirmations to me through the years has been the overwhelming support of my wife, Ruth. When I was working with the Youth For Christ organization or as pastor of a church, she always felt that God had given me the gift of an evangelist and that I must use it. She kept telling me so. And through the years she has given me wonderful support. Never once have I ever heard a word of complaint come from her lips about my being gone for long periods of time, or about the tremendous load that she had to carry in taking the major responsibility of rearing our five children. The evangelistic ministry in behalf *of* the saints is affirmed *by* the saints.

Third, the church confirmed the call by setting Paul apart for that ministry (Acts 13:1-4). Their Spirit-led action was endorsed by subsequent evidence. His evangelistic gift was apparent to all, both in Damascus (Acts 9:19-30) and in Antioch (Acts 13:1-3).

My first major pastorate was at the First Baptist Church of Western Springs, Illinois (a suburb of Chicago). I hadn't been there six months before at least three of the deacons told me that they felt God had given me the gift of an evangelist.

So Paul's ministry had a solid foundation, clear and definite confirmation, and a lifetime of evidence.

Now, the evangelist's prime responsibility is to preach the "Word." We must tell people, simply and clearly, what God says concerning His Son Jesus Christ, what He has done for all, their eternal destiny and need of salvation, and the urgency of accepting and receiving Jesus as their own personal Lord, Savior, and Master. Evangelists are not just to tell people *about* the Bible, but to proclaim it and communicate its message of salvation (2 Timothy 4:2-5). Very little originality is permitted a Western Union messenger. His sole obligation is to carry the message he receives from the office to the person to whom it is addressed. He may not like to carry that message — it may contain bad news or distressing news for the person to whom he delivers it. But he dare not stop on the way, open the envelope, and change the wording of the telegram. His duty is to take the message.

The primary concern of the evangelist is those who do not know Christ. The pastor and teacher focus on those who are Christians, but the ministry of the evangelist is directed to those who have never committed their lives to Jesus Christ as Savior and Lord. God may also use the evangelist to challenge Christians and bring renewal and rededication to them — but his primary goal is to win and seek to persuade the lost to a saving knowledge of Christ (see Ephesians 4:11–12).

But there's another goal that may be even more important. I remember years ago there was a missionary to Taiwan who had been a great American Bible teacher. He once taught at Wheaton College. He said, "Billy, your main purpose in an evangelistic effort is to vindicate the righteousness of God."

The evangelist's effectiveness depends primarily on two things. First, it is dependent on the clear and authoritative preaching of the Gospel message based on Scripture. "God says," and, "Jesus says," are more telling than "I think," "we believe," or, "our church teaches." Even secular observers and reporters note that my sermons are sprinkled with the phrase, "The Bible says . . ." I make no apology for this. God's Word is the source of my authority in proclaiming the Gospel. It is more powerful than human personality or natural ability. It is always living and active and relevant (Hebrews 4:12).

Second, the evangelistic message focuses on the cross where Jesus died, as man's substitute, for sin. The cross is foolishness to the mind of unregenerate man, but it is the power and the wisdom of God to those who are being saved (1 Corinthians 1:18,23–24). The evangelist should read widely. He should be informed on and familiar with the issues of the day and the concerns of those to whom he ministers. I read not only local American papers, but three British newspapers and several news magazines to try to keep abreast of the events of the day in various countries of the world. I have been to sixty-two countries to preach the Gospel, and I try to keep up with developments in each of those countries as best I can. I want to be an informed evangelist. When I go to different countries, I need to know something about their current situation. This helps me in my proclamation. But an effective messenger proclaims the Word and focuses on the cross.

The preaching of the Word must also be seen as distinctive. It is distinguished from that part of an evangelistic program used to attract attention to and prepare the way for the preaching of the Gospel. God used Jesus' miracles to confirm that He was indeed the promised Messiah. This is something like the way He uses testimonies of people whose lives have been transformed by the new birth.

Music also has a strategic ministry in preparing the hearts of unbelievers to listen to the evangelist. It is my great privilege to have had with me for well over thirty-five years Cliff Barrows, George Beverly Shea, and Tedd Smith. Cliff Barrows is in full charge of our music. I make suggestions to him from time to time, but it is largely his part of the service. He feels that music is a ministry to the people, as well as a preparation of the hearts for the message to follow. When George Beverly Shea sings, he sings a message. That's the reason people do not feel like applauding when he finishes singing — just as they don't applaud when I finish preaching.

In America in recent years so many young people are coming to the crusades, and they have a tendency to applaud — far too much, in my judgment. It may be the generation gap between them and me! Applauding is their way of expressing "Amen," as a congregation in America used to say after a good message.

It is the preaching of the Word — its exposition, its explanation, its illustration, its relevance to man's needs, and the world today — that is effective. This preaching is used by the Holy Spirit to convict of sin and bring saving faith (see John 16:8–11; Romans 10:17).

The extent of this responsibility is to all peoples. God places us where He needs us, but our ministry need not be limited to any one group, caste, or race. God does not discriminate among people. On the other hand, some are aware of special evangelistic gifts for working with children, young people, or perhaps a particular ethnic group. Peter's ministry was primarily to Jews, but it did not stop him from obeying God by going to a Gentile called Cornelius (Acts 10). Paul was given the task of preaching the Gospel to the Gentiles (Galatians 2:7–9), but such a powerful testimony could not help but influence his fellow Jews also.

We must understand that the Gospel message is powerful wherever and to whomever it is preached. It can reach the hearts of all, so that ultimately this supracultural and supernatural Gospel may extend to the thousands of unreached peoples of the world. It is God's message. We are His mouthpieces, responsible for the opportunities He gives us to share it with all who will hear. No person is inferior or to be ignored, for God wants "all men to be saved, and to come unto the knowledge of the truth" (1 Timothy 2:4). If there are those around us whom we consider inferior, God may have to deal with us and bring us to repentance so we begin to see them the way He sees them. "For the love of Christ constraineth us; . . . Wherefore henceforth know we no man after the flesh" (2 Corinthians 5:14,16).

Neither are we to be intimidated by those who, by the world's standards, may be counted superior to us. Peter and John were bold in their witness before antagonistic religious leaders (Acts 4). Paul was unashamed and powerful in his presentation of the Gospel to King Agrippa, without being disrespectful or impolite (Acts 26).

A friend of mine, now with the Lord, said, ''We need men and women who have this balanced attitude and conviction — people who are humble before God, and are aware that their power comes from His indwelling Holy Spirit, but who are confirmed in their minds that God has given them a high calling as His ambassadors.''

With all respect and good grace we are to share the Gospel. Be ready always (2 Timothy 4:2). God may use us to preach to great crowds, but He also needs our availability to share Christ with individuals such as a waiter, someone we may meet when traveling, a person He brings within our sphere of influence to hear the Gospel on a one-to-one basis. On one occasion God directed Philip away from a series of evangelistic meetings for a personal encounter with an influential Ethiopian who was led to Christ (Acts 8:26–39).

It is God who, by His Spirit, opens the hearts of all who are responsive to His Word (Acts 16:14).

But God wants to use us as His instruments to bring the Word to others — and He will, as we respond to His call to do the work of an evangelist as He directs.

There also has to be boldness. There have been times in my ministry when I have been tempted to compromise, water down, and lower the standard of the Gospel in order not to offend certain dignitaries who might be present.

God taught me through several experiences many years ago that I am never to do that. For example, I remember in 1954 we were at the Wembley Stadium in London. It was the end of a twelve-week Crusade that God had wonderfully blessed. One hundred and twenty thousand people were present, with many turned away (it was the largest audience in the history of Wembley). A number of the nobility of Britain were present, both on the platform and in the Royal Box. Sitting by my side was the Archbishop of Canterbury, Dr. Geoffrey Fisher. Three months earlier only one assistant bishop had stood with us and little attention had been given to the preparations of the Crusade; but now three months later, because God had so gloriously blessed, a great many of the leaders of the country were there.

As I looked at that audience and at the people on the platform, I was tempted to change my message. I was going to preach on Joshua 24:15: "Choose you this day whom ye will serve," and I thought to myself, "This is far too simple a Gospel; what will these great leaders think of such a simple message preached extemporaneously?" I'd had very little chance to prepare the message, because three or four hours earlier we had preached at the White City Stadium to sixty thousand people, and I was feeling the effects of three months of preaching. But the still, small voice inside said, "No. I gave you this text and you are to preach on it no matter who is here." So I got up and preached it. I felt a great power and a great boldness. And when the invitation was given, many hundreds responded. When the Archbishop of Canterbury walked down the steps from the platform, he said to one of my colleagues, "I suppose we'll never see a sight like that again until we get to heaven!"

God had honored the preaching of His Word.

Affirmation IV

—— ⟡ ——

I read aloud the fourth Affirmation:

God loves every human being,
who, apart from faith in Christ,
is under God's judgment and
destined for hell.

The response was:

I affirm.

—— ⟡ ——

God's love is far beyond human comprehension.
Finite man can never fully understand its infinite nature. Yet the Bible stresses that love is part of the
nature of God. The Bible says, "God is love" (1 John
4:8).

We see something of the depth of God's love when
we remind ourselves that He is the Creator of everything — including us. We are not here by accident —
God created us in His image and made us so that we
could have fellowship with Him. The psalmist declared, "When I consider thy heavens, the work of thy
fingers, the moon and the stars, which thou hast ordained; What is man, that thou art mindful of him?
and the son of man, that thou visitest him? For thou
hast made him a little lower than the angels, and
hast crowned him with glory and honor" (Psalm
8:3–5). He created us in His image and He cares for us
every day — because He loves us. This is why God

created man. "God is love" (1 John 4:8). He created man because He wanted creatures in the universe who could return His love voluntarily. Without being irreverent we could almost say that God was lonely. He wanted others with whom He could fellowship. They would love Him because they *chose* to love Him. Thus He created man in His own image. This does not mean that God created man in His physical image, but in His spiritual and moral image, such as mind, emotion, and will. The body is designed for giving expression to the spiritual and moral nature of man. God created man so that man would be capable of fellowship with Him.

But we see the true depth of God's love for us when we look at the cross. He loved us so much that He was willing to send His only Son into the world to die for our sins. In that awful moment, when Jesus died on the cross, He was enduring more than just the physical pain of the nails in His hands and feet and the crown of thorns in His head. He was enduring the awesome agony of hell itself — separation from God His Father — as He took upon Himself our sins and our death and our judgment (see Matthew 27:46; 2 Corinthians 5:21).

In the Apostles' Creed there is a phrase that is often left out in modern editions of the Creed: "He descended into hell." In a spiritual and literal sense Jesus did descend into hell, taking our hell and judgment upon Himself. (Incidentally, this is the only explicit mention of the atonement in the Apostles' Creed and should never be left out in reciting it.) Because He was the Son of God, He had the capacity to endure all the pangs of hell for everyone who was to believe and follow Him — in the generations past and in the generations to come. Only in that way could salvation be won, and only in that way would we be judged, and yet saved.

The best-known verse in the Bible summarizes this profound truth clearly, "For God so loved the world, that he gave his only begotten Son, that whosoever believeth in him should not perish, but have everlasting life'' (John 3:16). That is the depth of God's love for us — that He sent His Son to die for us. As Paul stated, ''For scarcely for a righteous man will one die: yet peradventure for a good man some would even dare to die. But God commendeth his love toward us, in that, while we were yet sinners, Christ died for us'' (Romans 5:7–8).

Are you sometimes tempted to doubt God's love for you, or wonder if He has abandoned you and does not care? Look at the cross and realize that if you had been the only person in the world who needed redemption, He still would have died for you because He loves you. ''Hereby perceive we the love of God, because he laid down his life for us: ... In this was manifested the love of God toward us, because that God sent his only begotten Son into the world, that we might live through him. Herein is love, not that we loved God, but that he loved us, and sent his Son to be the propitiation for our sins'' (1 John 3:16; 4:9–10).

But there is another side to God's character. God is a God of love, but He also is a God of justice. He is just, because He is holy. What if sin always went unpunished? Would God be holy if He allowed the world to be filled with sin and rebellion and never did anything about it? No! His holy nature demands that sin be punished. ''Thou art of purer eyes than to behold evil, and canst not look on iniquity'' (Habakkuk 1:13). His holy, perfect nature also means that His justice is always perfect as well.

We must keep both of these biblical truths in balance (see Romans 11:22). There is no conflict between God's love and God's justice when we understand them correctly. In Jesus Christ and His death on the cross *the judgment* and *the love of God* come together (see Psalm 85:10). We must never stress God's love so much that we lose sight of His justice, and make the error of thinking God could never punish sinners who reject Him. We must never stress His justice so much that we lose sight of His love — a love so deep that God has provided for us a means of salvation.

Man's rebellion and fall in no way diminishes God's love. He doesn't stop loving us because of our sinful natures. But His nature is not only loving, it is also just. And He exercises justice impartially. So while His love is extended to the sinner, His justice demands severe judgment of sin.

Sin, like an infectious disease, has spread throughout the human race (Romans 5:12). Its root has been variously expressed as rebellion, selfishness, pride, egotism, and unbelief. The consequences or the "wages of sin" is death, both spiritual and physical (Romans 6:23). And yet God, in infinite grace and mercy, still loves us enough to provide a way for our salvation and the satisfaction of His justice (Romans 3:16-22).

I have heard evangelists as well as pastors preach on hell as though they were glad that people were going there. No one should ever preach on the subject of hell without tears in his or her eyes. It should be proclaimed with great compassion, and yet boldness.

None of us deserves God's love. All of us deserve His righteous judgment and wrath (John 3:18,36; Romans 3:9-12). It is easy to think of an evil and depraved man like Adolf Hitler deserving divine judgment. We may be able to name contemporary figures in the same category. But think of the kind and good people that you know — but because they too are sinners (though they may not be the worst kind), they still have come short of God's requirement for entrance into heaven. They too will be lost if they refuse and neglect God's offer of mercy and forgiveness. God's judgment applies to them too. The highest of human standards fall short of His righteousness (Isaiah 64:6).

So we dare not neglect to warn that there is a Judgment Day approaching (see Acts 17:31). There is a sense in which contemporary man recognizes this.

The secular world is talking more and more about Armageddon and the end of the world.

A British newspaper columnist wrote, ''The day of reckoning is near.'' An American government official said, ''Sometimes I get the feeling I am sitting on a hilltop watching two trains racing toward each other on the same track.''

But the judgment of God is not only an event that may take place some day in history when war or conflict might bring death to millions. His judgment is more than death — it is eternal banishment from the presence of God (2 Thessalonians 1:6–10; Revelation 20:11–15). Nevertheless, God can use the fear that grips the hearts of men today to point them to eternal truths — the truth of God's eternal judgment, and the truth of His eternal love.

This is a crucial time for the Christian evangelist to proclaim the hope of salvation that we have in Jesus Christ, and to emphasize that some day the prayer, ''Thy kingdom come. Thy will be done in earth, as it is in heaven,'' will be answered. The future does not belong to capitalism, communism, fascism, or any other ideology. It belongs to Christ and to those who follow Him. In the solemn light of that day of judgment, man's greatest need is for reconciliation to God.

With the background of divine judgment, God's love can be seen in better perspective. It is at the center of our evangelistic message, symbolized by a cross silhouetted against a Middle Eastern sky. God sent His Son to reveal His love. He suffered and died to prove it. The judgment we rightly deserve was borne by Jesus on the cross (1 Peter 2:24). How God's love could be so great that it reaches down to sinners and makes them sons and joint-heirs with Jesus (Galatians 4:4–7) we can never understand. But it is, and that is what He did.

Hell is not the most popular of preaching topics. I don't like to preach on it. But I must if I am to proclaim the whole counsel of God. We must not avoid warning of it. The most outspoken messages on hell, and the most graphic references to it, came from Jesus Himself. He spoke of hell as "outer darkness" where there will be "weeping and gnashing of teeth" (Matthew 8:12; 24:51; 25:30). He contrasts "everlasting punishment" with "life eternal" (Matthew 25:46). He describes hell as a place of torment and agony and fire (Luke 16:23–24).

Jesus used three words to describe hell. The first is "darkness." The Scripture teaches that God is light (1 John 1:5). Hell will be the opposite. Those who have rejected Christ will go into outer darkness (Matthew 8:12). The second word He used to describe hell is "death." God is life. Man is separated from the life of God and endures eternal or the second death. The third word that He used is "fire." Jesus used this symbol over and over. This could be literal fire, as many believe. Or it could be symbolic. God does have fires that do not burn. And also there is the figurative use of fire in the Bible. For example, in the epistle of James we read that the tongue "is set on fire of hell" (James 3:6). That doesn't mean that the tongue has literal combustion. I've often thought that this fire could possibly be a burning thirst for God that is never quenched. What a terrible fire that would be — never to find satisfaction, joy, or fulfillment! God takes no delight in people going to hell. He never meant that anyone would ever go to hell. He created it for the devil and his angels (Matthew 25:41). But those who persist in going the devil's way and obeying the devil instead of God are going to end up in hell.

Even John, the apostle of love, wrote, "And whosoever was not found written in the book of life was cast into the lake of fire" (Revelation 20:15). Paul, in his great sermon to the intellectuals of Athens, declared that God "commandeth all men every where to repent: Because he hath appointed a day, in the which he will judge the world in righteousness by that man whom he hath ordained" (Acts 17:30–31).

If the Bible so clearly records this punishment of unbelievers, we dare not dilute it. To make it a symbol or a myth is to rob the cross of its glory and distort the immense love of God. And it reflects in the ministry of the evangelist by reducing his passion for the lost. No wonder there is a lack of urgency in the ministry of those who avoid this subject, or who fail to accept its reality.

The lostness of man is more than separation from God. It is more than straying and being unable to find the way back to the Father's home. It is more than an absence of the life of God — even eternal life or abundant life — in the individual. All these are true, but the unbeliever and the disobedient need to be warned of the final consequences of their rebellion. They need a preacher, an evangelist, who will tell them the whole truth so they may be "delivered . . . from the power of darkness" and brought "into the kingdom of his dear Son" (Colossians 1:13).

The Bible, from beginning to end, is the story of God's love. So the seriousness of hell must not be masked. It cannot be avoided. Evangelistic integrity demands that we dare not hide it.

Faith in Christ is God's alternative to judgment and hell. In Jesus is help, hope, and eternal life. Those who lived before Him, who trusted in the promise of the Messiah, were saved. "Abraham believed God, and it was counted unto him for righteousness" (see Genesis 15:6; Romans 4:3). So also those of us who live because of the fulfillment of God's promise in sending Christ are saved by faith (Ephesians 2:8). Forgiveness and salvation are free gifts to those who receive them by faith. Restoration to fellowship with God is the result. Believers who are "in Christ Jesus" are assured of "no condemnation" (see John 5:24; Romans 8:1).

We evangelists should be throwing the lifeline to those who are drowning; we should be giving the bread and water of life to those who are spiritually hungry and thirsty. We have a Savior to proclaim to a lost and dying world which stands under God's judgment.

Affirmation V

I read the Affirmation:

The heart of the biblical message is the good news of God's salvation, which comes by grace alone through faith in the risen Lord Jesus Christ and His atoning death on the cross for our sins.

The response came back:

I affirm.

※

Salvation is always "good news." It is news of God's love and forgiveness — adoption into His family — fellowship with His people — freedom from the penalty of sin — liberation from the power of sin. It brings God's plan and direction into our lives. We have the privilege of serving Him which gives meaning even to the most menial tasks. We also have the exciting anticipation of Christ's return — the answer to His prayer, "Thy kingdom come. Thy will be done in earth, as it is in heaven."

Nothing can compare with all that is ours in Christ when we are "born again." Forgiveness — justification — adoption — eternal life, and heaven too. What a glorious life we have to offer through the Gospel to those who are searching for purpose and meaning in life; or to those who have been crushed by oppression or circumstances; or to those who have found that materialism and sensual pleasure are not the answer to the deepest yearnings of their heart.

The crowning glory of salvation is promised when we enter into the presence of the King (1 Corinthians 2:9–10). We have a home in heaven reserved for us and awards which await us (John 14:1–3; 1 Peter 1:3–5).

No wonder the Gospel is "good news." What a privilege we have to proclaim it! I can think of no higher calling than to be an evangelist — a bearer of this good news of eternal life to those who are dying.

That doesn't disqualify us from suffering. Peter, who wrote so eloquently about the future prospects of the believer, seemed to question his present situation when he reminded the Lord that they had left everything to follow Him. Jesus, in turn, reminded Peter that while God does reward His children in their present situation, He does not promise trouble-free lives (Mark 10:28–31). In fact, Scripture affirms "all that will live godly in Christ Jesus shall suffer persecution" (2 Timothy 3:12). But beyond all this is the promise of eternal life and all it implies.

Unfortunately, many persons today have distorted the meaning of biblical salvation, saying that it means only political, social, and economic liberation in this life. Certainly, Christians should be concerned about injustice, and do what they can within their societies to promote a more just world. But lasting and complete liberation from social injustice will come only when Jesus Christ returns to establish His Kingdom. Biblical salvation is far deeper, because it gets at the root of man's problem — the problem of sin. Only Christ can change the human heart and replace greed and hate with compassion and love.

Those of us who are called to be evangelists must be clear about the content of the Gospel we proclaim. A person should understand certain truths before he can make an intelligent commitment to Jesus Christ. What is this "heart of the biblical message"? What must we proclaim if people are to comprehend God's plan of salvation?

I always have certain points in every evangelistic sermon that I feel I must cover no matter what text I take, or what outline I use, or what illustrations I may give.

First, we need to emphasize that all are sinners and stand under the judgment of God. "For all have sinned, and come short of the glory of God" (Romans 3:23). A person may believe that he is good enough to win God's favor, or think that he can perform certain religious acts to counterbalance his bad deeds. But the Bible states that we are all condemned, for "there is none righteous, no, not one" (Romans 3:10). Furthermore, sin has consequences, both in this life and in eternity. "How shall we escape, if we neglect so great salvation" (Hebrews 2:3). As John Wesley said, "I must preach law, before I can preach grace." People must be aware that they have broken God's law before they can realize their need.

Second, we need to emphasize what Christ has done to make our salvation possible. God loves us, and Christ came to make forgiveness and salvation possible. What did He do? He died on the cross as a complete sacrifice for our sins. He took upon Himself the judgment that we deserve (1 Corinthians 1:21–25; 2:1–5; 15:1–4). The message of the cross must be central in our preaching.

Third, we need to emphasize what a person must do in response to God's work in Christ. God in His grace offers us the gift of eternal life — but like any gift, it becomes ours only when we reach out and take it. We must repent of our sins. Repentance (*metanoia* in Greek, meaning a change of mind) carries with it the idea of confession, sorrow, turning, and changing. *The New Bible Dictionary* defines it as "a radical transformation of thought, attitude, outlook, and direction" (see Acts 2:36–38; 20:21). We cannot ask forgiveness over and over again for our sins, and then return to our sins, expecting God to forgive us. We must turn from our practice of sin as best we know how, and turn to Christ by faith as our Lord and Savior. "For by grace are ye saved through faith; and that not of yourselves: it is the gift of God: not of works, lest any man should boast" (Ephesians 2:8–9). Christ invites us to come to Him, and God has promised, "as many as received him, to them gave he power to become the sons of God, even to them that believe on his name" (John 1:12).

Fourth, we must emphasize the cost of coming to Christ and following Christ. Jesus constantly called upon those who would follow Him to count the cost. There is a cost in repentance. A person must determine to leave his personal sins behind and turn from them, and some persons may be unwilling to do so. But there may be other costs as well when a person decides to follow Christ.

The ultimate cost to true discipleship is the cost of renouncing self: self-will, self-plans, self-motivations. Now Christ is to be Lord of our lives, not the old self-centered sinful nature. Jesus declared, "If any man will come after me, let him deny himself, and take up his cross daily, and follow me" (Luke 9:23). Jesus does not call us to a life of selfish comfort and ease — He calls us to a battle! He calls us to give up our own plans and to follow Him without reserve. Repeatedly in the New Testament people are called to turn to Jesus not only as Savior but as Lord (Romans 10:9–10; 14:9). We are not saved by our good works — but by the same token we are called to follow Christ in trust and obedience (Romans 1:1–5; 6:17). "He that hath my commandments, and keepeth them, he it is that loveth me: and he that loveth me shall be loved of my Father" (John 14:21).

Yes, it costs to follow Christ — but it also costs *not* to follow Christ. It cost Paul the prestige and security of a high-level position in the Jewish nation — but he declared, "What things were gain to me, those I counted loss for Christ. Yea doubtless, and I count all things but loss for the excellency of the knowledge of Christ Jesus my Lord" (Philippians 3:7-8). On the other hand, the rich young ruler wanted to follow Christ — but when he realized he would have to put Christ in first place, instead of his wealth, "he went away sorrowful" (Matthew 19:22). And Christ did not stop him or lower His standards. Some of the intellectuals of Athens refused to turn from their false philosophies and religions to follow Christ, saying to Paul, "We will hear thee again of this matter" (Acts 17:32). But so far as we know, the opportunity never came again. The Roman governor Felix listened to Paul and came under deep conviction for his sins, but he refused to repent and follow Christ, saying, "When I have a convenient season, I will call for thee" (Acts 24:25). The "convenient season" never came, and Felix, so far as we know, died apart from Christ.

Let us always remember that Christ calls men and women not only to trust Him as Savior, but also to follow Him as Lord. That call to discipleship must be part of our message if we are to be faithful to Him. As The Lausanne Covenant states, "In issuing the gospel invitation we have no liberty to conceal the cost of discipleship."[1]

The salvation we offer, in Christ's name, is intimately linked to the cross. The man who hung there between two thieves was without sin. His virgin birth, by the miraculous intervention of the Holy Spirit (Matthew 1:20), meant that He did not inherit a sinful human nature. Neither did He commit any sin during His lifetime (1 Peter 2:21-22; 2 Corinthians 5:20-21; Hebrews 4:15). Mary gave birth to the only perfect child. He became the only perfect man. As such, He was uniquely qualified to put into action God's plan of salvation for mankind.

Why was Calvary's cross so special, so different

from hundreds of other crosses used for Roman executions? It was because on that cross Jesus suffered the punishment for sin which we all deserve. He was our substitute. He suffered the judgment and condemnation of death that our sinful nature and deeds deserve. "For he hath made him to be sin for us, who knew no sin; that we might be made the righteousness of God in him" (2 Corinthians 5:21).

That was the purpose of the cross — Jesus, the sinless One, substituted Himself for us sinners. We, who are sinners, "become the righteousness of God"! We cannot become more righteous than that. We cannot receive anything better in life. God has given us salvation through His Son. We receive it by grace — unmerited — undeserved (Romans 6:23).

The apostle Paul wrote to the church at Corinth, "I determined not to know any thing among you, save Jesus Christ, and him crucified" (1 Corinthians 2:2). Paul knew there was a built-in power in the cross and the resurrection. It has its own communicative power. Paul well knew that the Holy Spirit takes the simple message of the cross, its redemptive love and grace, and infuses it into lives with authority and power.

I well remember a meeting early in my ministry when I walked away from where I was preaching, disheartened and disappointed. A businessman who was with me at the time asked me if I knew what was wrong. But I couldn't put my finger on it until he told me. "Billy," he said, "you didn't preach the cross!" He was right. The message had been theologically sound, and I had preached it as best I knew how. But that vital ingredient was missing. I learned my lesson. From that day to this, I have never preached an evangelistic message without pointing those listening to the cross.

Faith is another essential for salvation. The evangelist must be absolutely clear on what he means when he preaches salvation "by faith."

There are various kinds of belief or faith, and not all

are linked to salvation. Faith in the New Testament means more than intellectual belief — it involves trust and commitment. I may say that I believe that a bridge will hold my weight — but I only believe it when I commit myself to it and walk across it. It is possible to believe in the life and death of Jesus in history, but faith in the historical record of Jesus is no more saving faith than believing the historical record of Julius Caesar. Even Satan believes — in fact, he knows beyond any shadow of doubt — that biblical history concerning Jesus is true (James 2:19). But he is still condemned. Then there is a kind of theological faith which may begin in Sunday school. It believes that Jesus died for sinners. This is a statement of truth about God that makes even the demons in hell shudder, yet doesn't lead them to saving faith. Saving faith involves an act of commitment and trust, in which I commit my life to Jesus Christ and trust Him alone as my personal Savior and Lord.

Let me use a personal example to illustrate this. When I first met Ruth, my future wife, I began to learn things about her — born in China, the daughter of medical missionaries, and so on. As time went on, I learned more about her personality and character, and I fell in love with her. But we were not yet married. We became husband and wife only when we took a definite step of commitment to each other on our wedding day.

In the same way, saving faith is a *commitment* to Jesus as Savior and Lord. It is a personal and individual decision. It is more than assent to historical or theological truth given to us in God's Word. It is faith in the promises of God as the believer's only hope for eternal life (John 5:24; 1 John 5:10–11).

This is the good news we preach.

Affirmation VI

✥

I read publicly the Affirmation:

In our proclamation of the Gospel we recognize the urgency of calling all to decision to follow Jesus Christ as Lord and Savior, and to do so lovingly and without coercion or manipulation.

The response came:

I affirm.

✥

Every time I give an invitation I am in an attitude of prayer — because I know the situation is totally dependent on God. Incidentally, this is the moment in a meeting when I feel emotionally, physically, and spiritually drained. This is the part of the evangelistic service that often exhausts me in every way. I think one of the reasons may be the strong spiritual battle going on in the hearts of so many people. It becomes a spiritual battle of such proportions that sometimes I feel faint. There is an inward groaning and agonizing in prayer that I cannot possibly put into words. I am sure every true evangelist senses this.

Urgency is another ingredient of this aspect of the evangelist's ministry. Of course, whenever we preach, there is a sense of urgency in the message, but this comes to a climax at the moment of invitation. The urgency I feel at that time is compelling. I know there could be many who, if they leave without making their commitment to Christ, may never have another opportunity like this again. When the call for decision has been made and many are responding, I still feel a continuing sense of urgency for those who are holding back. I've felt the same urgency as I've shared Christ with an individual on a plane, or in an office. Urgency is an indispensable part of the work of an evangelist.

The urgency in calling people to a decision is based on three concerns. First, Jesus taught that there is an eternal destiny for each individual — either heaven or hell (John 5:25-29). The eternal destiny of each individual depends on a decision made in this life (Luke 16:19-31) — to be followed by a life of obedience. No decision for Christ can be made after death. "It is appointed unto men once to die, but after this the judgment" (Hebrews 9:27).

Second, we have no assurance of continued physical life tomorrow (see Proverbs 27:1). There is an urgency to the Gospel because life can end at any moment. Someone to whom we speak may never have another opportunity to hear the Gospel and accept Christ. "Behold, now is the accepted time; behold, now is the day of salvation" (2 Corinthians 6:2).

Third, a delayed decision can result in a heart that becomes hardened to the call of God's Spirit. The Bible warns us about being "hardened through the deceitfulness of sin" (Hebrews 3:13). The Bible also warns, "He, that being often reproved hardeneth his neck, shall suddenly be destroyed, and that without remedy" (Proverbs 29:1). So the evangelistic message always contains a note of urgency born out of the teaching of Scripture.

This urgency is expressed by the evangelistic call to all who hear the Gospel. This call is an integral part of the evangelist's responsibility; he does not merely preach truth but proclaims it with a view toward some of his hearers responding positively to the Gospel. Of course, the Gospel must be simply and understandably communicated, the issues made plain, the necessity of a response — positive or negative — clearly taught. At that point the evangelist is dependent on the power of the Scripture and the ministry of the Holy Spirit to work in and through the message in the hearts of all who hear.

While the evangelist is essentially a harvester, his message may be used by God in another way. It may be a preparation of some hearts for a subsequent positive response — a planting of the seed of the Gospel. For others, it may be a watering of that seed which leads to decision. God is sovereign and we cannot dictate to Him the stages through which He may choose to bring an individual to saving faith. Paul wrote, "I have planted, Apollos watered; but God gave the increase. So then neither is he that planteth any thing, neither he that watereth; but God that giveth the increase" (1 Corinthians 3:6-7).

The call to decision is scriptural. It is found repeatedly throughout the Bible. It begins with God calling Adam and Eve (Genesis 3) when they hid from Him because of their sin. It ends with God's call by His Spirit through His witnesses and evangelists, "The Spirit and the bride say, Come. And let him that heareth say, Come. And let him that is athirst come. And whosoever will, let him take the water of life freely" (Revelation 22:17).

The Word of God is a re-echoing invitation to lost humanity to turn to Him.

Moses issued an invitation when he said, "Who is on the Lord's side? let him come unto me" (Exodus 32:26).

Joshua appealed to Israel to make a definite commitment, "Choose you this day whom ye will serve" (Joshua 24:15). When the people said they would decide for God and serve Him, Joshua wrote it down and had a great stone set up as a witness to their decision.

Elijah confronted the false prophets of Baal and the unbelief of the people on Mount Carmel. In 1 Kings 18:21 we read that he challenged the people, "How long halt ye between two opinions? if the Lord be God, follow him: but if Baal, then follow him." All through Scripture, God is giving people a choice. In 1 Kings 18:30 we read that Elijah gave his invitation, "And Elijah said unto all the people, Come near unto me. And all the people came near unto him." When God miraculously consumed the sacrifice on the altar, the people responded, "The Lord, he is the God; the Lord, he is the God" (1 Kings 18:39).

Isaiah records God's call to sinful Judah, "Come now, and let us reason together" (Isaiah 1:18).

The same prophet invites those who are thirsty to "come ye to the waters," and, "Seek ye the Lord while he may be found, call ye upon him while he is near" (Isaiah 55:1,6).

John the Baptist preached in the wilderness, and multitudes came to hear him and respond to his call for repentance.

Jesus said to Peter and Andrew, "Follow me, and I will make you fishers of men" (Matthew 4:19).

At Pentecost Peter called the people to repentance (Acts 2:38) and three thousand responded. (Someone must have counted them!)

The apostle Paul wrote to both Jews and Gentiles, "For whosoever shall call upon the name of the Lord shall be saved" (Romans 10:13). And to the church at Corinth he wrote, "Knowing therefore the terror of the Lord, we persuade men" (2 Corinthians 5:11). The word "persuade" in Greek is a strong word — carrying with it the idea of "strong persuasion."

But we must be careful that coercion does not enter into that persuasion. The Bible's urgent call can be abused by some well-intentioned evangelists. Gifted personalities have the ability to excite emotions and manipulate people. Others can use dubious means, such as threats, scare tactics, and psychological pressure to make "converts," or become so anxious for numbers that the invitation is broadened to include any person or problem. In some countries I found that I could have the entire audience come forward, if I did not know their cultural and religious background. They will just take Jesus and add Him to the many other gods that they have. We have to be specific. I believe that invitations should be clear and straightforward if we are to be faithful to the Gospel. Paul declared, "We ... have renounced the hidden things of dishonesty, not walking in craftiness, nor handling the word of God deceitfully; but by manifestation of the truth commending ourselves to every man's conscience in the sight of God" (2 Corinthians 4:1-2). I never ask people to raise their hands — and then later ask them to take the additional step of coming forward. I make it a straight out, uncomplicated call for public commitment and witness.

We have heard all kinds of "explanations" of why people come forward in our crusades. In London, England, one newspaper reporter claimed that it was the emotional effect of the music (the hymn "Just As I Am") that caused people to come. So on some evenings we stopped having any music when the invitation was given. Even more people came forward in the hushed silence of the huge arena. After the first night that we cut out the music, a reporter said it was the "emotional silence" that caused them to come! Naturally, the reporter knew very little about the work of the Holy Spirit.

I am convinced that a high-pressure invitation cannot be the call of God the Holy Spirit. By such methods we can be guilty of giving people a false assurance of salvation. That's leading them astray, and leaving them in a worse situation than before. Also, we may build great resentment against the Gospel.

Finally, there are men with great personal charisma and personality who can induce people to follow them — instead of Christ. Some who began as servants of Christ have become sidetracked by their own egos. Jesus never asked us to make disciples to ourselves, nor even to our church or denomination — as good as these may be. John the Baptist declared concerning Jesus, ''He must increase, but I must decrease'' (John 3:30). The person who is most used by God is the person who has learned the secret of standing in the shadow of the cross, pointing to Christ instead of himself.

We are commissioned to make disciples, to bring them into the same direct relationship with Christ as those who left their nets and their fishing boats to become ''fishers of men.'' When we go to a city for a Crusade, I recognize that hundreds of people have participated in prayer and the preparations for the Crusade. Therefore I, as the evangelist, cannot take credit for the results. It is the work of people being used by the Holy Spirit in different capacities. It is teamwork. For example, in all the work that we do I have a team of people with me. Jesus sent them out two by two. They were a team of people. No one person could take the credit. While a great deal of the publicity may surround my name, and I often cringe from it, yet I recognize that in this day of advertising it probably has to be done. But Billy Graham did not win these people to Christ. Almost every person who comes to Christ is a result of many factors in his life. When we get to heaven, we may be surprised by the different ways souls are counted and claimed, as against our methods on earth. The evangelist is extremely important, but so are those who support him and surround him and help him.

The work of evangelism could be likened to the links in a chain. No link is more important than the other. Even the last link cannot take precedence over the first. Ultimately, God alone saves, but not without the links in the chain of witness, prayer, and faith. He has chosen, in His sovereignty, to work that way. How wonderful to be able to say with the great apostle, ''We are laborers together with God'' (1 Corinthians 3:9).

Affirmation VII

I read the following seventh Affirmation:

We need and desire to be filled and controlled by the Holy Spirit as we bear witness to the Gospel of Jesus Christ, because God alone can turn sinners from their sin and bring them to everlasting life.

More than four thousand replied,

I affirm.

In the previous Affirmation we noted that we are to proclaim the Gospel ''without coercion or manipulation.'' The reason we do not need to try to force people to believe is that God is at work through the Holy Spirit when the Gospel is proclaimed faithfully. We, therefore, are to trust Him to accomplish His purposes in the hearts of those who hear the Gospel.

The Holy Spirit is the great Communicator. Without His supernatural work, there would be no such thing as conversion. Satan puts a veil over the truth, and this can be penetrated only by the power of the Holy Spirit. It is this Third Person of the Trinity who takes the message and communicates with power to the hearts and minds of men and women. He breaks down the barriers. He convicts of sin. He applies the truth of the Gospel we proclaim. No evangelist can have God's touch on his ministry until he realizes this reality and preaches in the power of the Holy Spirit. We, as proclaimers of the Gospel, must understand that the natural man cannot accept the truth of Christ. The things of God are foolishness to him. He cannot understand them because they are spiritually discerned (1 Corinthians 2:14).

That is why Jesus said, "When he [the Spirit] is come, he will reprove the world of sin, and of righteousness, and of judgment" (John 16:8). We can — and must — preach the Gospel, but in the final analysis it is the Spirit who interprets the Word to the hearer and quickens it. We cannot manipulate His sovereign work; and once we understand that the results are in God's hands, it will give us freedom from anxiety and fear of failure. Jesus told Nicodemus, "Except a man be born of water and of the Spirit, he cannot enter into the kingdom of God. ... The wind bloweth where it listeth, and thou hearest the sound thereof, but canst not tell whence it cometh, and whither it goeth: so is every one that is born of the Spirit" (John 3:5,8). Yes, there is a mystery to the working of the Spirit — but we know that God alone can turn sinners from their sin, and bring them to everlasting life.

Again, Jesus explained, "It is the spirit that quickeneth; the flesh profiteth nothing: the words that I speak unto you, they are spirit, and they are life" (John 6:63).

The filling of the Spirit was a prerequisite for power in the ministry of the first evangelists (Acts 1:8). Their Spirit-filled witness began in Jerusalem, then spread to Judea and Samaria, and on to the ends of the earth.

The Spirit's filling does not "guarantee" the results we would like to see. Peter's preaching at Pentecost resulted in three thousand who "gladly received his word" and "were baptized" (Acts 2:41). Peter was equally filled with the Holy Spirit (Acts 4:8) when he later preached to a more select group. No converts are recorded here — only antagonism, bewilderment, and persecution. Saul (Paul) was filled with the Holy Spirit when he rebuked Elymas, the sorcerer. The apostle correctly prophesied the sudden blindness of this enemy of the Gospel. This resulted in the proconsul of Cyprus believing (Acts 13:8–12).

We need to be filled with the Holy Spirit — but what exactly does that mean? Some define it in terms of certain experiences or feelings. But the New Testament stresses that when we are filled with the Spirit we are *controlled* by the Spirit.

The apostle Paul illustrates this when he commanded, ''Be not drunk with wine, wherein is excess; but be filled with the Spirit'' (Ephesians 5:18). Instead of being controlled by the wine of the world, we are to be controlled by the Spirit of God. Instead of devil intoxication, it must be divine intoxication. The verb is the present passive imperative — which implies a yieldedness to the Holy Spirit's control. As we yield so He fills; as He fills so He controls. This may be a quiet, unemotional reality — in fact, at times we may not even be conscious of it. But when we are filled with the Holy Spirit, we renounce our dependence on ourselves and our own strength, and yield ourselves to His control. As we commit our lives to the Lordship of Jesus Christ each day, the Spirit of God fills us and empowers us for the work God has for us.

The Spirit-filled life is the normal Christian life. It enables the evangelist to speak the Word of God with boldness. When the early Christians received threats that might have diminished their boldness, they had special prayer for a fresh in-filling. God granted their request and, once again, they ''spake the word of God with boldness'' (Acts 4:31).

My wife has often reminded me that I should always preach from an ''overflow.'' I know what she means. To be so filled with Scripture and so filled with the Holy Spirit that day or night I can give a reason for the hope that is within me, or give a Bible exposition, or give an evangelistic sermon (see John 7:38–39; 1 Peter 3:15).

I remember many years ago sitting on the platform in the Moody Church in Chicago. At that time I was an evangelist for Youth For Christ. Actually, I had become the first employee of Youth For Christ International and was serving as an evangelist. As I was sitting on the platform, Dr. Harry Ironside was to deliver the message. He was one of the greatest Bible-teaching evangelists I have ever heard. He knew the Scriptures from end to end and could preach on any occasion without a note. I remember sitting there, and I noticed the song service was a bit long, and I saw that the good doctor (who was getting along in years) was sound asleep. When his time came to speak, someone nudged him; he woke up, stepped up to the podium, opened the Bible, and preached a powerful message. He preached from an overflow.

This Spirit-filled life was not an option for the early church, neither is it an extra for today. It is essential. The Holy Spirit's ministry is an indispensable requirement to enable people to be "born of the Spirit."

There is another reason for the evangelist to know the fullness and control of the Holy Spirit. He will encounter supernatural opposition. Beyond human opposition to our work, we can expect spiritual forces of evil (Ephesians 6:12). The "prince of the power of the air . . . now worketh in the children of disobedience" (Ephesians 2:2). That's why we cannot convert anyone. We cannot match the power of Satan, but we do have authority over him when we call on the power of God's indwelling Spirit. The supernatural opposition we face is also one reason why one of the most important aspects of evangelism is prayer.

In his letter to the Ephesians Paul clearly indicated that the evangelistic ministry is a fight, not a frolic. And he realized the need of supportive prayer by God's people. Paul sought intercessors, prayer partners, among the Ephesian Christians who would pray in the Spirit on all occasions with all kinds of prayers and requests (Ephesians 6:18). "Praying . . . for me," he continued, "that utterance may be given unto me, that I may open my mouth boldly, to make known the mystery of the gospel" (Ephesians 6:18–19).

Sometimes I have been asked the "secret" of our worldwide ministry which has continued for so long. It is not the organization, as important as it is to do things "decently and in order." It is not the publicity and media coverage, as valuable as these are in extending the influence of the Gospel. It is not the special talents or gifts of our team, nor my preaching. I am convinced that in heaven credit for all that has been accomplished in the power of God's Holy Spirit will go to those hundreds of thousands of Christians who are faithful in prayer for us. They have the most essential part in our ministry. As I preach the Gospel, they pray, as Paul asked of the Ephesians, "that . . . I may speak boldly, as I ought to speak" (Ephesians 6:20).

The apostles certainly understood the Holy Spirit to be the Third Person of the Godhead — not an ethereal influence but a Person, who is an essential part of evangelism. Their evangelistic task would have been impossible without His indwelling and control.

The Spirit-filled life enables the evangelist to be used of God. It is essential that we recognize the difference between being used *of* Him and of our attempt to use God. To try to use God in accomplishing even our most noble ambitions will lead to frustration and ultimate failure.

Seeming lack of success in our objectives, even when we are controlled by the Spirit, is something we may experience in our evangelistic ministry. Paul, Silas, and Timothy had plans to continue preaching the Word in Asia. But the Holy Spirit prevented this. We're not sure how, but the same thing happened when they tried to enter Bithynia. God had another plan for them, in Macedonia (Acts 16:6–10). There

need be no contradiction between good, careful planning and the Holy Spirit's leading. Yet we are to be
flexible and open to circumstances beyond our control
as well as to that quiet, persistent conviction that the
Holy Spirit is leading us to a place and to a people He
has prepared.

I remember many years ago plans were made for
me to address a meeting in an East European country.
There was great excitement and keen anticipation. But
then twenty-four hours before going, there was clear
direction both to me and the organizers that I should
not go. There was no time to stop people traveling
from all over the country to attend the meeting. There
may have been some human disappointment at my
not being there, but it did not hinder the working of
God's Holy Spirit. The place was packed. The preaching of a local evangelist was powerful. God's Spirit
moved and many came to Christ. God had another
plan for me at that time, but years later he allowed me
to preach in that city and see great blessing.

Finally, the servant of God knows when he is not
spiritually prepared to proclaim the Gospel because he
has grieved the Holy Spirit by committing sin (Ephesians 4:30). Maybe bitterness has crept into his life, or
envy of Christians who seem to have greater blessing.
It could be jealousy concerning another evangelist
who appears to be more successful. Or anger. Or
unkindness. His prayer life may have suffered and
Bible reading been neglected.

Each of us will experience times of testing. None
of us is immune. We may be stuck on a spiritual
plateau — instead of pressing on to the mountaintop.
There may be times when we don't feel like preaching.
Even when that which is wrong is confessed and forgiven and cleansed (1 John 1:9), we may be called to
walk by faith, not by feeling, as we minister. Some of
our most effective service may be accomplished without a consciousness of having been successful and
effective.

God rewards the faith we place in the power of the Spirit to use Scripture and bless the witness of even the weakest vessel. His Word will not return empty but will accomplish that which He desires and achieve the purpose for which He sends it (Isaiah 55:11).

Constantly, and in all humility, we need to remind ourselves that "except the Lord build the house, they labor in vain that build it" (Psalm 127:1).

Is your life controlled by the Spirit of God? Or has some sin crept into your life and clogged the channels of His blessing? Turn to Christ for cleansing, and yield your life without reserve to His Lordship. Then in constant dependence upon the Holy Spirit, let Him use you for His glory to touch other lives for Christ.

Affirmation VIII

⚜

I read aloud the affirmation:

We acknowledge our obligation, as servants of God, to lead lives of holiness and moral purity, knowing that we exemplify Christ to the church and to the world.

They responded:

I affirm.

⚜

Preaching is not the only way we declare the Gospel of Christ. Our lives also should be witnesses to others of the reality of Christ. Those who have affected me most profoundly in my life have not necessarily been great or eloquent preachers, but men and women of God whose lives were marked by holiness and Christ-likeness. The Gospel must be communicated not only by our lips but by our lives. This is a visual proof that the message we preach actually can change lives.

Our world today is looking for men and women with integrity, for communicators who back up their ministry with their lives. Our preaching emerges out of what we are. We are called to be a holy people — separated from the moral evils of the world. The Bible commands, ''As he which hath called you is holy, so be ye holy in all manner of conversation'' (1 Peter 1:15). The apostle John wrote, ''Love not the world, neither the things that are in the world. If any man love the world, the love of the Father is not in him. For all that is in the world, the lust of the flesh, and the lust of the eyes, and the pride of life, is not of the Father, but is of the world. And the world passeth away, and the lust thereof: but he that doeth the will of God abideth for ever'' (1 John 2:15–17).

It seems to me that an evangelist, and the clergy for that matter, especially faces temptation in three areas: pride, money, and morals. There were also three areas of temptation reflected in the verse we have just quoted: first, the lust of the flesh; second, the lust of the eyes; and third, the pride of life. These areas are appeals to misuse natural appetites. These are exactly the areas of appeal that Satan chose to tempt Eve in Genesis 3:4–6 and Jesus in Matthew 4:1–11. Eve yielded to the temptations; but our Lord Jesus Christ, through being filled with the Holy Spirit and quoting the Word of God, overcame Satan's temptations. Jesus stated, ''Ye are the light of the world. . . . Let your light so shine before men, that they may see your good works, and glorify your Father which is in heaven'' (Matthew 5:14,16). Peter urged, ''Having your conversation honest among the Gentiles: that, whereas they speak against you as evildoers, they may by your good works, which they shall behold, glorify God in the day of visitation'' (1 Peter 2:12).

Standards of life-style and conduct for those in the Christian ministry are rooted in the Old Testament patriarchs, leaders, and prophets. They were approved by God for the way they lived. That did not mean they were perfect. The Bible is absolutely honest about their sins and failure. It records these, sometimes in embarrassing detail, so that we may learn from them and avoid their failures (Romans 15:4).

Jesus Himself received God's approval, for as a man He experienced the same real temptations of all mankind; yet He was without sin (Hebrews 4:15). He remains for us the model of holiness and moral purity.

Early in His ministry, in the Sermon on the Mount, Jesus taught His disciples about the narrow gate and the difficult road that leads to life (Matthew 7:13-14). He warned against false prophets. Good trees, He said, produce good fruit, but bad trees cannot produce good fruit. Then He warned His disciples about those who, in His name, prophesy (or evangelize), drive out demons, and perform miracles, but do not put His Word into practice. They will be rejected. They will not enter the kingdom of heaven (Matthew 7:15-23).

Peter and Jude warned against false teachers, who are corrupted by sensuality, greed, immorality, and ungodliness (2 Peter 2; Jude). The test of true faith is expressed by an inward quest for godliness in all areas of life. We are to be holy as God who called us is holy; we are to be set apart for Him in all our behavior.

Even though Timothy was a young man who seems to have occupied a pastoral ministry, the apostle Paul exhorted him to be ''an example of the believers, in word, in conversation, in charity, in spirit, in faith, in purity'' (1 Timothy 4:12). Again, in his second letter to Timothy, the apostle reminded him of his holy calling, a unique service for God which called for an exemplary life (2 Timothy 1:6-9; 2:1-26).

In his letter to the Ephesians Paul warned, ''But fornication, and all uncleanness, or covetousness, let it not be once named among you, as becometh saints'' (Ephesians 5:3). ''For God hath not called us unto uncleanness,'' he wrote to the Thessalonians, ''but unto holiness. He therefore that despiseth, despiseth not man, but God, who hath also given unto us his holy Spirit'' (1 Thessalonians 4:7-8).

In my travels throughout the world I have found that questions on different standards of conduct arise. Often these are largely cultural differences and have nothing to do with the basic moral issues. The most important thing is what God desires of us to please

Him and to be an example of Christ. With this as our objective we have a number of things to bear in mind.

First, apostolic standards of godliness and purity apply to us today. It is dangerous to interpret the Bible in such a way as to justify or excuse our sins, by saying some of its statements on behavior applied only to first-century culture. In this connection it is important to study a passage such as 1 Corinthians 10:1–15, and see how Paul applied the same principles on holy living that related to the children of Israel centuries before. Indeed, he said, "All these things happened unto them for ensamples: and they are written for our admonition, upon whom the ends of the world are come" (1 Corinthians 10:11). Thank God, he added, "There hath no temptation taken you but such as is common to man: but God is faithful, who will not suffer you to be tempted above that ye are able; but will with the temptation also make a way to escape, that ye may be able to bear it" (1 Corinthians 10:13).

Second, Jesus died on the cross for our sinful nature as well as for the sins resulting from it. With this in mind, we will want to stay as far away from sin as possible — not see how close we can come without getting caught. The story is told of a medieval king who wanted to find out who was the best-qualified man to be his chariot driver. Three men were chosen as the best in the realm, so he took them up to a high cliff and asked them to drive along the rugged road with a sheer drop of more than a thousand feet. The first two drivers drove as fast as they could and as close to the edge as they could, showing how skillfully they could maneuver the chariots even though they were close to the edge. The third driver drove fast, but he drove many yards away from the edge of the cliff. He was the one who was chosen.

In both of Paul's epistles to the young Timothy he counseled him to actually "flee" from temptation (1 Timothy 6:11; 2 Timothy 2:22). In other words, put as much distance as possible between yourself and that which the devil would use to destroy your testimony.

Third, some sins — such as pride, moral impurity, covetousness, jealousy, and anger — may be secret and hidden from others for a time. It may appear that all is well on the outside. But they destroy our inner man, so that we are unable to proclaim the Gospel with the liberty and power of the Holy Spirit. Samson lost his strength when he succumbed to Delilah, but he was not immediately aware of it. When the enemy came, he said, ''I will go out as at other times before.'' Then, in one of the saddest verses in the Old Testament, we read, ''And he wist not that the Lord was departed from him'' (Judges 16:20). How often we have seen a once powerful preacher, going out ''as before'' but not realizing that sin had robbed him of the power he had almost come to take for granted. It is a sad and tragic spectacle.

Fourth, each church knows its own cultural evils, those practices which belong to the old life before becoming new creatures in Christ (2 Corinthians 5:17). Yet even cultures and traditions can be flexible — but not standards of godliness, holiness, and moral purity in God's Word. These never change in any culture. Paul continually warned the different churches to which he writes of those who will not inherit the kingdom of God. The list includes those practicing fornication, idolaters, adulterers, sexual deviates, thieves, the covetous, drunkards, revilers, and swindlers (1 Corinthians 6:9–10; Galatians 5:19–21; Ephesians 5:5).

Fifth, some Christians look at another brother who does not indulge in their pet sin and call him a ''legalist.'' They don't realize that this virtually means adding our good works to the atonement. Others in this category are stronger on social piety than personal godliness. For example, it is easy to sit on a committee and vote help to the needy — but much harder to say ''no'' to a besetting personal sin, or to go out and personally engage in social work.

If something is specifically condemned in the Bible, such as sexual immorality, we can be in no doubt that it is wrong. Temptation, of course, is not a sin. It is yielding to the temptation that is sin. There are things in the Bible that are not actually named, but we know them to be wrong. A safe guideline was once given me when I was a student at Wheaton College. The president at that time, Dr. V. Raymond Edman, would advise, "If in doubt, don't do it. When in doubt, put it out."

Sixth, we need to realize that a person who is called to the ministry of evangelism is often subject to special temptations. This is due in part to the fact that Satan hates the proclamation of the Gospel and will throw his evil forces into the battle with special intensity in an effort to blunt the work of Christ. Satan will do all he can to get us to doubt, or compromise our message, or commit sin, or get sidetracked into minor issues. He will appeal to our pride to make us think we are self-sufficient and cause us to depend less on God. Remember the warning of Peter — who himself knew what it meant to fail and give in to Satan's temptations, "Be sober, be vigilant; because your adversary the devil, as a roaring lion, walketh about, seeking whom he may devour: whom resist stedfast in the faith" (1 Peter 5:8-9). That warning applies as much to the evangelist as to anyone else. The constant travel, the association with different people all the time, the temptations of being in the spotlight, the temptation of financial irresponsibility — these and many other things can cause the evangelist to sin and wreck his ministry. We are to lead lives of holiness and moral purity, knowing that we exemplify Christ to the church and to the world.

I have seen some tragic consequences of young evangelists who could not resist the temptations that we have mentioned. I remember one, when I first started out. He had a gift of evangelism beyond that of almost anyone else I have ever met or heard. He could sway and move great crowds. There was a great response to his ministry. But pride and ego became his stumbling block. This led to sexual immorality. Within five years he died a tragic death.

I know another man who also was extremely gifted. Cliff Barrows led singing for him for a while. He too could not resist the temptations of the world. He left his wife and children, ended up in the most horrible condition imaginable, and died a tragic death.

There are many through the years on several continents whom I could mention, who have been tripped up by Satan. It usually started with something that seemed innocent, but it led to deeper and deeper problems and greater and greater sin. Their ministry was destroyed, their families disillusioned or broken-hearted, and thousands of people hurt.

May God grant you the power of His Holy Spirit to resist all temptations, and particularly those that are peculiar and strong to an itinerant evangelist.

Affirmation IX

I read aloud the Affirmation:

A life of regular and faithful prayer and Bible study is essential to our personal spiritual growth, and to our power for ministry.

To which they responded:

I affirm.

Evangelists are activists. Traveling, meeting new people, organizing, and preaching keep us busy. But we need to remember that it is not so much our *activity* for Christ as our *captivity* for Him which is most important. My friend Dr. Stephen F. Olford warns preachers about ''the barrenness of a busy life.''

Many times I am asked if there are aspects of my ministry I would change if I were starting again. Throughout my ministry I've been under pressure to go to too many places and speak too much. My study time has suffered. If I had to do it over again, I would speak less and study more.

Prayer and Bible study are essential in the life of every Christian, but especially is this so in the life of an evangelist. It leads to liberty in Christ and joyous, rewarding service.

Not every evangelist will have the privilege of preparing for his ministry with formal biblical and theological training, as desirable as this is whenever possible. But at least he should get some good commentaries and a Bible dictionary by evangelical scholars so he can understand the Bible's meaning more fully. He also should strive to be simple in his presentation of the biblical message, so then even the person who has no background in the Gospel can understand it. I have found it sometimes takes greater work to be simple in a sermon than it does to be profound. Jesus set the example by giving the profoundest truths in utter simplicity, often using simple everyday illustrations to illustrate spiritual truth.

I remember giving a series of evangelistic lectures at Cambridge University some time ago. In the opening service I presented the Gospel as clearly as I knew how, though I tried to put it in what I thought was a student framework. The next morning in the discussion with the staff they were almost unanimous in saying that I had gone over the heads of the students. They felt that the students had a poor understanding of the Bible, and that I could not take anything for granted. They urged me to be even more simple in my presentation. Thus it took a great deal of rearranging of my sermon plans and also much more time spent in prayer.

I have a daughter who is a powerful Bible teacher and expositor of the Word of God. She gets up every morning at 5:30 to spend two hours on her knees in prayer every single day. There have come times when I felt that she was jeopardizing her health, but her spiritual power is so great that I hesitate even to mention it to her.

There is no substitute for fellowship with the Lord. Freedom in His service comes through the inner resources of power supplied by the resurrected Christ, indwelling us by His Holy Spirit (Colossians 1:27; Romans 8:1–11).

We should never forget that God Himself desires

our fellowship. "But the hour cometh, and now is, when the true worshipers shall worship the Father in spirit and truth: for the Father seeketh such to worship him" (John 4:23).

David, the warrior king of Israel, responded to the demands of leadership in this way, "One thing have I desired of the Lord, that will I seek after; that I may dwell in the house of the Lord all the days of my life, to behold the beauty of the Lord, and to enquire in his temple" (Psalm 27:4).

Power from a fresh, daily anointing of the Holy Spirit in the time you are alone with God is the product of a healthy devotional life. There is no shortcut to such power in the ministry. Nor do we ever reach a point in our ministries where this is no longer needed. When we give ourselves in evangelism, we must also receive from the Lord new resources, new growth, and renewed power. The further we go in our ministries, the greater the demands made on us and the more our need for strength — both physical and spiritual.

Prayer and Bible study are inseparably linked. Effective prayer is born out of the prompting of God's Spirit as we read His Word. When the apostles were persecuted, weary with their ministry and threatened by the religious authorities, they needed three steps to renewal. One, they considered the Scriptures. Two, they prayed. Three, they were filled afresh with the Holy Spirit. The result? They "spake the word of God with boldness" (Acts 4:31). This practice reinforced the principle taught by Jesus to the apostles, that the power of the Holy Spirit is essential for an effective witness to the resurrected Lord.

Someone said, "You're never preaching until the audience hears another voice."

So it is important to saturate ourselves in the Word of God, and our ministries in prayer. For the evangelist there is always the temptation to be sermon-hunting every time he opens the Word of God. But if this is all we do, then we easily neglect to feed and strengthen our own souls. We also overlook our own worship and praise of God. We must learn to come to the Word of God not just for what it will tell others, but for what it will teach us. We must learn to let the Word of God feed us and strengthen us in our faith in God its author, Christ its message, and the Holy Spirit its teacher.

We are encouraged to "grow in grace, and in the knowledge of our Lord and Savior Jesus Christ" (2 Peter 3:18). That is, we avail ourselves of the undeserved help and blessing God provides for us, and we learn more about His Son who is the central theme of the Bible. Such study brings greater maturity, greater stability, and greater discernment to speak the truth in love. By this growth in Christ we become of greater usefulness to His Body, the church. And as we grow spiritually, so our ministry grows. The alternative is to preach messages from dry wells, because we haven't studied sufficiently nor prepared adequately.

Faithful Bible study and prayer is never time wasted. The growing responsibilities of the early church in Jerusalem imposed greater demands on the apostles. Wisely, they delegated the additional work to others, saying, "It is not reason that we should leave the word of God, and serve tables. ... We will give ourselves continually to prayer, and to the ministry of the word" (Acts 6:2,4). An evangelist needs great wisdom and discipline to maintain that balance of study, prayer, preparation, and practical administrative work which is necessary to discharge his responsibility well.

In this connection, several practical guidelines have been helpful to me in maintaining a vital and regular time alone with God.

First, set aside time each day to spend time with God. It may be early in the morning, or at least before you begin the day's regular activities. Make it a time when you are mentally alert, when you have no distractions and you are not rushed. Discipline yourself to keep this time every day, even when travel or a busy schedule makes it difficult. Make it such a regular part of your life that you would no more skip it than you would miss eating a meal.

Second, come with a spirit of expectancy and obedience. Expect God to meet you through His Word, and tell Him that you want to be taught by Him. Come with a willingness to hear His Word and then to obey it. Remember: God the Holy Spirit has inspired the Bible, and we must look expectantly to Him to illumine our understanding of it.

Third, read through the Bible systematically. It is far too easy to dwell only on familiar passages, or skip around almost at random finding passages that happen to appeal to us. But we need to understand "the whole counsel of God" (Acts 20:27, RSV), and we need therefore to read and study every part of the Bible. Some people find it helpful to have a plan by which they will cover the entire Bible in a year.

Fourth, read thoughtfully and prayerfully, and then meditate on what you have read. Some people pride themselves on covering a set number of chapters each day — but have no idea what they have read when they are finished! In his helpful, little booklet "Manna in the Morning" Dr. Stephen F. Olford wrote, "Read the portion at least three times. Read it carefully to discover what is there generally. The next time, peruse it for what is there specially. Then study it for what is there personally. . . . [Then] say: 'Lord, as I look at this passage this morning, is there any command to obey? Is there any promise to claim? Is there any new thought to follow and pursue? Is there any sin to avoid? Is there any new thought about God? About the Lord Jesus? About the Holy Spirit? About the devil?' Seek to discover what God is saying to you from the passage you have read."[1]

Fifth, make prayer a central part of your time with God. In our Bible study, God speaks to us; in our prayer times, we speak to God. Make prayer first of all a time of praise and thanksgiving. Then pray about the passage of Scripture you have just read, asking Him to show you specific ways that it applies to your life. In addition, confess your sins to God. Finally, bring before God your own needs and the needs of others. Many people find it helpful to keep a prayer diary, in which they list those for whom they are praying and note God's specific answers.

Finally, put what you have learned into action, and walk with Christ every minute of the day. Perhaps God has been speaking to you in your quiet time about your relationship with someone in your family or a co-worker. Commit that situation into His hands — and then move forward in obedience and faith, knowing that the Holy Spirit will help you as you seek to have a right relationship with that person.

Our ministries are strengthened, sometimes more than we realize, by our devotional life. Our ability to explain great truths of Scripture with clarity and simplicity grows as they become a part of us and our experience. There is a sense in which the evangelist must not only possess the truth, but the truth must possess him. He will react spontaneously against sin and error rather than being slowly conditioned by it.

Methods and organization alone are not enough, important as they may be in their place. The reason is that we are involved in a spiritual battle. The evangelist and the work of evangelism are opposed on every hand by Satan and his forces. When the seed of the Gospel is being sown, Satan is always there sowing the tares and blinding the minds of those whom we seek to evangelize. Let us not underestimate the strategy of Satan. He uses every kind of deception, force, and error to try to destroy the effectiveness of the Gospel. So we must trust the Holy Spirit for the results in our evangelism because He alone can give success. And that is why prayer is such an important part of our work.

A life taught in the Scriptures, and tuned in to God in prayer, produces an outflowing of grace and power. "Put on the whole armour of God, that ye may be able to stand against the wiles of the devil. . . . Take . . . the sword of the Spirit, which is the word of God: praying always with all prayer and supplication in the Spirit" (Ephesians 6:11,17–18).

Stephen Olford has written on the quiet time:

"The quiet time is vital to *spiritual health,* whether you are newly converted or a mature Christian (see 1 Peter 2:2 and Hebrews 5:14).

"The quiet time is vital for *spiritual cleansing.* You are initially cleansed by the precious blood, that is true, and again and again you have to come back to the cross for restoration. But the day-by-day cleansing is from the laver of the Word (see Psalm 119:9; John 15:3; 17:17).

"The quiet time is also vital to *spiritual counsel.* You can never know the true principles that determine a life of holiness and righteousness without letting the Word of God 'dwell in you richly' (see Colossians 3:16 and Psalm 73:24).

"The quiet time is likewise vital in equipping you for *spiritual conflict.* The supreme example is our Lord Jesus Christ when He encountered Satan in the wilderness. I feel sure that for forty days and nights He had fed His soul on the book of Deuteronomy, and could therefore make His sword thrusts from a personal experience of the written Word.

"Paul later exhorted the believers in Ephesus to 'take . . . [unto them] the sword of the Spirit, which is the word of God' (Ephesians 6:17).

"Important as all these things are, however, the greatest incentive to your having a quiet time each day is not your own need, great as that is, but the fact that God wants to meet with you. Therefore, it is not merely a duty, it is a privilege and an honor.

"God in Christ, your Lord, has a trysting place with you. His heart is saddened when you fail to keep the appointment. He longs, as He did with the women of Samaria, to drink afresh of your love, devotion, and worship (see John 4:23–24).

"I would warn you that establishing your quiet time is never easy. As a minister, I will confess frankly that it is harder for me to have my quiet time now than it was when I was first converted. The reason for this is that what counts costs.

"You will find that the most vicious attacks of the adversary will be directed toward robbing you of that daily time with your Lord. And you will have to guard it fearlessly if you are to keep it.

"Whatever your sphere of service — as a pastor, Sunday school teacher, missionary, or Christian in the office or home — I give you little hope of living victoriously unless you are successful in maintaining your quiet time."[2]

Affirmation X

❦

I read aloud the Affirmation:

We will be faithful stewards of all that God gives us, and will be accountable to others in the finances of our ministry, and honest in reporting our statistics.

To which they responded:

I affirm.

❦

Someone has said, "The kingdom of God is not *built* on finances, but it cannot be *extended* without them." And in evangelism, money can be the source of many problems. At one end of the spectrum are evangelists who feel their ministries are limited by lack of financial support. At the other end are those whom God's people suspect of "making money" out of evangelism and even misusing funds.

Sadly, both can be true. That is why our stewardship of funds and our reporting of statistics need to be transparently honest. Even if others were not watching us and evaluating our ministries by what they see of our honesty and integrity, we still should be above reproach, because we are accountable to God. We are to "put on the new man, which after God is created in righteousness and true holiness'' (Ephesians 4:24). But the truth is that others judge us. More than that, they evaluate the truth of the Gospel by what they see of our lives and our integrity. Those engaged in evangelism — as well as those involved in any other type of Christian ministry — must make every effort to be above all suspicion in the matter of finances and statistics. We are not only accountable to God's people, but also to our Master (see Acts 24:16).

Jesus taught this in the parable about the use of money (Luke 19:11–27). Each servant received from the nobleman a sum of money to use for the good of their master's business. They were asked individually to give an account of what they had done with the funds entrusted to them. Each was rewarded according to what he had done with it. This aspect of an evangelist's work is an immense privilege, but it is accompanied by an awesome responsibility.

Many see the apostle Paul as a rugged individualist who believed himself to be responsible to God alone. But Scripture indicates that first he earned the confidence of the church by his submission to it and his service to it. From the early days of his conversion he submitted to the disciples, to Barnabas, and to the brethren of Jerusalem (Acts 9:25,27,30). Their confidence in him grew. He was sent with a gift for the famine relief of Christians in Judea (Acts 11:27–30). And the Bible carefully records that he and Barnabas fulfilled the mission (Acts 12:25). Even then, though, we see that two men were sent.

It seems that there were financial profiteers even in the New Testament church. But Paul could testify with a clear conscience, ''For we are not as many, which corrupt the word of God: but as of sincerity, but as of God, in the sight of God speak we in Christ'' (2 Corinthians 2:17).

The writer to the Hebrews gives both a warning and a wonderful promise, ''Let your conversation be without covetousness; and be content with such things as ye have: for he hath said, I will never leave thee, nor forsake thee'' (Hebrews 13:5).

Early in our ministry I sought the advice of several Christian leaders about steps I might take to avoid any possible misunderstandings about the finances of my ministry. At their suggestion the Billy Graham Evangelistic Association was incorporated. Its affairs are controlled by a dedicated board of directors, consisting of men and women who are experienced in business affairs and have deep Christian wisdom. All financial affairs are in their hands; I have no control over this aspect of the work. Along with the other evangelists on our staff, I am paid a salary by the board of directors. I have not accepted a personal gift, honorarium, or offering for my ministry in many years. Our finances are audited by a respected accounting firm, and their annual audited report is printed and made available to our supporters each year.

I realize that this procedure will not be possible for every evangelist. Every evangelist, however, should be deeply sensitive to the need for complete integrity in finances and should find some method of accountability so there can be no grounds for criticism.

I knew an evangelist several years ago who would take the offerings in his meetings and put the money in a suitcase in the trunk of his car. He gave no accounting to anybody. He did not even pay taxes on it. He harmed his ministry and he will some day have to answer to God!

The same principle of integrity must also apply to our reporting of statistics. Unfortunately some evangelists have not been as truthful as they should have been in reporting such things as total attendance or the number of people who were inquirers. This should not be the case. We should feel no need to exaggerate statistics, if we are truly seeking God's approval rather than building ourselves up in the eyes of men. One reason we began keeping statistics in our ministry was that we discovered that some news reporters were constantly publishing inaccurate and inflated statistics. As a matter of integrity, we determined to be absolutely honest in such matters.

In Proverbs 24:28 the Scripture says, "Deceive not with thy lips." The Septuagint translates it, "Overstate not with thy lips." Many years ago when Cliff Barrows and I were starting out in evangelism, we went to see an elderly evangelist to get some advice. He startled us with his advice to give statistics doubling the size of the crowds. He said, "People think you are exaggerating anyway, so exaggerate!" We came out of his office with a sinking feeling, and a terrible disappointment in a man whom we had looked up to.

We determined from that moment never to fall into that trap. We gave instructions to those who handle our statistics to underestimate if there is any doubt. Then we later came to the point of taking what the stadium officials said, or the police said, and reducing it by ten percent in our public releases. In the last twenty-five years I cannot recall one instance where we have ever been accused of exaggerating an audience. We don't need to — and in addition, it is wrong! I am always delighted to go to stadiums where turnstiles are used, and an actual count is given. And it is always interesting that the turnstiles indicate a much larger attendance that we would have estimated. For example, when we were in the Los Angeles Coliseum, the estimation of the officials and our Team was several thousand below what the turnstiles indicated. The last service of a month-long Crusade turned out to be the biggest audience in the history of the coliseum. They have a marker indicating that it was the largest crowd that was ever, or will ever be, there because they were able to use the playing field and thousands were outside who could not get in.

In Brazil we were in the Maracaña Stadium, which is the largest football stadium in the world. They cleared the moats of the water and brought in more people than the stadium could possibly hold, and still thousands were outside. The turnstile count was much higher than we probably would have given.

With smaller audiences we have had the people actually counted so that there could be no doubt. We strive for integrity in statistics.

One evangelistic group went to a certain country and had a large crowd to hear them proclaim the Gospel. The estimate of the crowd by the evangelist's team was double that of the actual number which was being counted by their hosts on computers. The team from America discharged the people who were counting them on computers and used their own estimates. This left a bad taste in the mouths of their hosts, but also was a discredit to the Gospel.

In some parts of the world I have found that exaggeration is an accepted and expected practice — but that does not make it right! We have had to argue, and sometimes were misunderstood, because we insisted on accuracy.

We also have done the same thing concerning the people who respond to the invitation. For a long time we did not give any statistics, but we found that the newspapers were exaggerating the number coming forward because they counted counselors too. Thus we had to issue accurate statistics. We do not call them "decisions," we call them "inquirers." We cannot possibly tell what is happening in the human heart even though the invitation may be clear, straight, strong, and difficult. Yet we know that the parable of the sower applies to all of those who respond. We know that many will fall away and could not possibly be counted as decisions. I have found through the years that it pays a thousand times over to strive to be honest. Naturally there will be mistakes, but they should be honest mistakes.

Accountability in the ministry of the evangelist extends far beyond financial or statistical matters. In the divine plan of revelation and redemption even

Jesus is seen reporting back to His heavenly Father concerning His mission and earthly ministry.

The issue of faithful stewardship was faced by the apostle Paul in relation to the congregation at Corinth. Division in the church could have led him to compete with Apollos over converts. This would have aggravated existing tension. But he handled things wisely by pointing out that while he planted and Apollos watered, any numerical increase was due to God (1 Corinthians 3:6). It is God, he says, who rewards faithful stewardship.

He takes nothing from Apollos' ministry, but he does warn that evangelists should be careful how they build on the solid biblical foundation laid by another. It is our sacred responsibility to be faithful stewards (1 Corinthians 3:10).

He concludes that servants of Christ — and we might add especially itinerant evangelists — should establish trustworthy reputations. The role of evangelists is strategic in the mission of the church. They should be able to trust one another and earn the confidence of all believers (1 Corinthians 4:1–2).

Paul's good conscience before the Lord enabled him to warn the Corinthians about accusing him of wrong motives in his ministry. As evidence, he pointed to the humble circumstances of his life, his weakness, lack of honor, hunger, thirst, poor clothing, rough treatment, hard work, and persecution (1 Corinthians 4:3–13). He is an example of both faithfulness to God and accountability to the church.

The world and some Christians sometimes incline toward suspicion of those in the public eye who are entrusted with funds. Even though some abuse the confidence of God's people, it is wise and biblical to report with integrity. This is true both of financial matters and statistics on results of attendance and response, ''that in the mouth of two or three witnesses every word may be established'' (Matthew 18:16).

Affirmation XI

---⟱---

I read aloud the Affirmation:

Our families are a responsibility given to us by God, and are a sacred trust to be kept as faithfully as our call to minister to others.

To which the response was:

I affirm.

---⟱---

The family seems to be a special target for satanic attack these days. Christian families are by no means immune. And the peculiar pressures on an evangelist's family make it particularly vulnerable. That's why he should consider ministry to his own family as *the most important part of his calling.*

Evangelists' wives carry burdens unique to this vocation. An evangelist should not do itinerant work without the full support of his wife. The apostle Paul's general admonition to all Christian husbands is especially applicable to evangelists when he writes, ''Husbands, love your wives, even as Christ also loved the church, and gave himself for it'' (Ephesians 5:25).

Children too are a heritage from the Lord (see Psalm 127:3). Those of the evangelist's family will be subject to pressures peculiar to their parents' calling. In most cases husband and wife are united in their response to the call to an evangelistic ministry, even if the wife's part is to stay at home. They are volunteers in the Lord's army. But their children are *conscripts*. They did not choose to be the sons and daughters of an itinerant evangelist, so we must lovingly respect their situation and raise them to appreciate rather than resent their role (see Ephesians 6:4; Colossians 3:21).

It is important that lines of communication between the evangelist and his family are always open. Aware of the fact that my own family sacrificed ''quantity'' of time with me, I have tried to compensate with ''quality'' of time. And however busy I was, my study door was never closed to the children. We have five children, and with thanksgiving, and praise, and glory to the Lord — and to Ruth — they are all dedicated believers.

Children are a gift from the Lord. They are to be reared with love and firmness. The Christian parental hope and prayer is that they may be the kind of example which will cause their children to reverence the Lord.

Christian parents are responsible not only for the physical needs of their children — which even nature teaches — but also for spiritual growth (Deuteronomy 6:4-9; 32:45-47). Verbal instruction should be accompanied by example. If they see you do something that is contrary to your preaching or testimony, they will lose confidence in your Gospel. I met a businessman several years ago whose father was one of the best-known pastor/evangelists in North America. He had five sons. Not only did his sons fail to follow in their father's footsteps, but they had all gone away from the Lord. I can imagine the grief and suffering of that father's heart through the years. Whether he and his wife were at fault, I do not know. But the businessman son who sat by my side said, ''My father preached wonderful messages, but he did not live them out at home.''

If our children hear us talking about honesty and

yet fail to see it in our lives, this inconsistency will do great harm. If we talk about God as a loving heavenly Father, and yet we are stern, unloving, or insensitive to our children, should we be surprised if they grow up doubting that God loves them?

A teenager once complained, "The problem with parents is that by the time you get them, they're too old to change!"

No parents are perfect. There will be problems, but the important thing is to build mutual understanding with our children. Love must be evident when correction is necessary. It is a happy husband-wife relationship and their evident oneness in Christ that leads children toward faith in Him and makes for a happy, wholesome family life.

Paul, writing to Timothy, gives the strongest possible admonition and warning to husbands and fathers, "If any provide not for his own, and specially for those of his own house, he hath denied the faith, and is worse than an infidel" (1 Timothy 5:8). The provision referred to need not be confined to material things, but also to time and energy and concern.

One evangelist was made aware of this when he was thumbing through his diary one evening. His young son, seeing the small book by which his father's life was ordered and controlled, said, "Daddy, could you put my name in there?"

This eleventh Affirmation is a simple recognition of the biblical institution of the family (Genesis 2:18,24). By implication it also draws attention to the sacred nature of the marriage vows. The permanence of the union cannot be overstated. The strong prohibition of adultery in the Ten Commandments and the death penalty imposed by the Old Testament civil law for Israel on adulterous living laid the foundation for the high regard of the family in the New Testament. The sacred bond of the marriage relationship is upheld by statements of Jesus, and the apostolic warnings about fornication and adultery are solemn and severe. The

Bible says that they who live like this "shall not inherit the kingdom of God" (1 Corinthians 6:9; see Galatians 5:18–21).

Most of us are aware of unfortunate and unhappy situations in Christian families. But God's loving concern for the welfare of His church — and for a nation — requires responsible leadership in family life.

For many years I used the book of Proverbs daily. (Its thirty-one chapters provide daily readings for a month.) I've gone back to doing that, because it is packed with sound instruction for moral integrity within marriage and wisdom in parenthood. Love, firm discipline, and a godly example are the ingredients of God-honoring family relationships.

Paul taught Timothy that church leaders must be those who manage their own household well and have control of their children (1 Timothy 3:4). Titus is instructed that a church leader must "be blameless, the husband of one wife, having faithful children not accused of riot or unruly" (Titus 1:6). These standards certainly apply to leadership in evangelism as well.

Demands on the itinerant evangelist are great, but I would suggest three practical pointers toward family responsibility.

First, understand there is no conflict of responsibility with God. The work of an evangelist and the demands of family life are not irreconcilable to Him. Any problem lies within us. Often a godly concern for those without Christ and the urging of others for our ministry make it difficult for us to refuse invitations to preach. Prayerful examination of every request in light of our responsibility to our families is important. We must not feel guilty when we give our wives and children the consideration they deserve. This has been one of my own problems. As I look back over my life, I see that I have made many mistakes. One of them was accepting too many nonrelevant invitations to the detriment of time with my family. The Lord has gloriously overruled, but if I had my life to live over again, I would spend a great deal more time with my family.

It took me years to learn that I do not have to accept every invitation to speak. Sometimes God would have me say "no" to invitations that seemingly are important and provide great opportunities — but are not so important as spending time with my family.

Second, in itinerant evangelism we are separated from our families a great deal. It is imperative that we give our wives and children additional attention when we are home. If we feel responsible for the material and physical welfare of our families, we should be equally sensitive to their needs for moral and spiritual leadership.

Third, there are sacrifices peculiar to itinerant evangelists. Many begin this work when single and do not fully consider the implications this has in married life. Evangelists planning to marry should pray for a capable and unusually equipped life partner. In retrospect, I know that only the Lord could have chosen Ruth for me and led us together. She has had to carry so much responsibility alone. She has shared the burden of my ministry. I cannot imagine any other woman who could have handled being Mrs. Billy Graham the way she has. God equipped her for this role, and without her love for the Lord and for me, and her dedication to the ministry of evangelism, I would not have been able to function for the Lord as I have.

There was a young girl who was brought up in a pastor's home where she knew nothing but poverty — not enough money for clothes, not enough money for food, not enough money for fun. She built up a growing resentment against her situation. At the same time, she did everything that was expected of her in the church — she taught Sunday school, played the piano, and did everything else that was expected of the pastor's daughter. Then when she was in her late teens, an older man fell in love with her and she was delighted not only because she was in love with him, but also because she thought, "Now is my chance to get out of the rat race of this whole poverty." The man was a businessman and had a good job. Shortly after they were married, he was called into the ministry, and she was back in the same old rut: not enough money to do the things she wanted. The growing resentment mounted so severely that after the children were raised and in college, she decided that she would take her own life. She carefully prepared her suicide so that it would look like a natural disaster.

The night before she was going to commit suicide, they happened to turn on the television, and one of our Crusades was on. When the invitation was given, she heard her name! (Sometimes I say during the invitation, for example, "Bill, Mary, John — you must turn your life over to God. He will help you to handle your problems.") She felt the invitation was speaking directly to her. She didn't want to do anything at home, so she stumbled over to the little church, knelt beside one of the pews, and poured out her heart to God. She realized that He loved her, and she was flooded with the sense of His love and His forgiveness and His total acceptance. As a result, she became a new person. She totally accepted the role which He had given her in life, and she has become a radiant and devoted wife of a pastor.

Every wife is different, of course; for some the fear of being alone while her husband travels on an evangelistic campaign is almost more than she can bear. There must be honesty and open communication in facing this; the evangelist must be sensitive to her needs and feelings. He may need to take practical steps to help her, such as involving others in his local church more deeply in the life of his family, while he is away. So I say to evangelists — strive to help your wife spiritually also, so that she will fully share your vision for reaching others for Christ and be a full partner in your ministry.

The Lord knows our needs in this important area of life. He knows that a mistake could spell disaster and an end to a promising evangelistic ministry. Pray that *His* choice will be yours.

God enable us to be both effective itinerant evangelists and worthy family leaders for His glory.

Affirmation XII

❦

We are responsible to the church, and will endeavor always to conduct our ministries so as to build up the local body of believers and serve the church at large.

I affirm.

❦

Many times the evangelist is regarded as a maverick — someone doing his own thing, building his own "empire," establishing his own following — and not placing enough emphasis on the church as a whole or the local bodies of believers where he ministers. In many cases, such views are accurate. Constructive criticism is justified. Proclaiming Christ must be linked to building His church, the importance of which is clearly taught in the New Testament.

The apostle Paul points out that the purpose of the gifts of apostle, prophet, pastor, teacher, and *evangelist* is "for the edifying of the body of Christ" (Ephesians 4:12). And he goes on to explain, "From whom the whole body fitly joined together and compacted by that which every joint supplieth, according to the effectual working in the measure of every part, maketh

increase of the body unto the edifying of itself in love"
(Ephesians 4:16).

The first recorded indication of the importance of
the church to Jesus comes in discussion with the men
He later commissioned as the first itinerant evangelists. When Peter declared, "Thou art the Christ, the
Son of the living God" (Matthew 16:16), Jesus responded, "Upon this rock I will build my church"
(Matthew 16:18).

Proclamation of who Jesus is and the building of
His church are clearly linked. Pentecost launched the
apostles into a ministry of proclamation that began to
build Christ's church. Repeatedly in the Acts of the
Apostles we read references to the numerical, struc-
tural, and geographical expansion of the church (Acts
2:41; 5:14; 6:7; 11:26).

This building of the church was obviously an apostolic concern. There was definite recognition of the
spiritual nature of the church as Christ's Body, but the
New Testament also places great importance on the
visible expression of this in local congregations. The
epistles were generally written to one or more of these.
And Paul, as an itinerant evangelist, concerned himself strongly with the welfare and progress of the
churches he planted (such as the one at Philippi) and
those begun by others (such as the one in Rome).

Why was this the case? Paul was not interested in
building an elaborate organization. Paul was interested in seeing people come to Christ, and then grow
in Him. He knew that Christ's Great Commission was
not just a command to get people to become believers,
but to teach them "to observe all things whatsoever I
have commanded" (Matthew 28:20). Paul understood
the church was vital in God's plan, for it was the place
where God's people could worship and grow spiritually. Paul wrote, "Christ also loved the church, and
gave himself for it" (Ephesians 5:25). It is normal,
therefore, for the evangelist to love the church that
Jesus loves. Such love will begin with, and transcend,

the local church, and even legitimate and rightful denominational loyalty.

For the evangelist, responsibility to the church begins in fellowship with the local church. This may be the church that first recognized and encouraged his evangelistic gift. It should certainly be a church which gives him prayerful and practical support. Ideally, it will also provide a caring spiritual home for his wife and family, particularly when he is away. He should, if possible, be a member of that church; and, as far as his ministry allows, should be active in it, attending when he is able and supporting it financially. In this way the evangelist is seen to be a man who submits himself not only to God's authority directly, but also to the authority of pastor(s) and the church.

The responsibility of the evangelist to the church continues in his preparations for an evangelistic campaign. I have made it a practice in my ministry never to go into a city for a campaign unless I have first been invited by a group of churches. We have always sought to work as closely as possible with churches in all phases of Crusade preparations. One reason for this is that we want to challenge as many Christians as possible to become active witnesses to Jesus Christ, and an evangelistic campaign is often an excellent opportunity for this. Time after time we have seen churches revitalized because of their participation in an evangelistic effort.

A further aspect of the evangelist's responsibility to the church is that the fruits of an evangelistic ministry which serves Christ should be directed to biblically based churches that cooperate in the outreach. The evangelist should recognize, support, and encourage the pastors of churches where he works. Planting churches in new areas should not be in isolation from existing churches but wherever possible associated with them.

Paul saw evangelism as the spearhead of the outreach of the local church when he wrote, "Having hope, when your faith is increased, that we shall be enlarged by you according to our rule abundantly, to preach the gospel in the regions beyond you" (2 Corinthians 10:15–16).

There can be some confusion between church-oriented evangelism and building God's kingdom in a broader sense. But there need be no dichotomy here. Those who come to Christ enter His kingdom immediately. It simply means that through the new birth they make Jesus King of their lives (John 3:3,5–7). With this vertical relationship comes a horizontal ministry when their lives in the community reflect a loving and caring concern for others. More than that, they, like Abraham, are strangers and pilgrims on earth looking forward to a better country, a city God has prepared. So while children of the kingdom have a future hope of that which is to come, they recognize their earthly responsibilities here and now. So Christ gathers a people for His name, the "called out" ones who unite in the church to worship Him. Viewed in this way, the church and the kingdom are two different perspectives of the one program of world evangelization.

The visible body to which the evangelist is responsible, for which he conducts his ministry, and to which he directs its fruits, is the local church. In this regard he must be faithful to the Lord Jesus Christ and to His Word.

I was reared in the Presbyterian church, but through a series of circumstances became a Baptist. Nevertheless, I do not go around the world proclaiming the Baptist faith, or the Presbyterian faith. I feel that as an evangelist I represent all the denominations and all the churches that are supporting the campaign. I try to avoid non-essential issues that divide churches. By non-essential I mean issues that are not essential for salvation. Naturally, I proclaim the Gospel with boldness, and there are some churches that feel they cannot support such a campaign. They may not believe in evangelism. Others may feel that cooperating with all kinds of churches is compromise. Therefore some of their pastors do not feel free officially to support the campaign.

However, I have found that in most cities to which we go, about eighty percent of all churches support the campaigns. There is a great tide running in many countries toward evangelism. I believe conferences such as the ones in Berlin, Lausanne, Pattaya, Amsterdam, and elsewhere and the ongoing work of the Lausanne Committee on World Evangelism have contributed to this rising interest. I also believe that our identification with church leaders of many denominations has also contributed to a better understanding of the work of the evangelist and the work of the church.

In this connection I would like to repeat something I said in Amsterdam. I think the church, through the years, has been wrong in not recognizing the gift of the evangelist as much as the gift of the pastor or the gift of the teacher. These are all gifts of the risen Lord to the church (see Ephesians 4:7–13). But the gift of the evangelist has often been neglected by the church. At the same time, in reacting to this, the evangelist himself has often failed to cooperate with the church.

Let us do the work of an evangelist, helping to build the Body of Christ.

Affirmation XIII

ॐ

I read the Affirmation:

We are responsible to arrange for the spiritual care of those who come to faith under our ministry, to encourage them to identify with the local body of believers, and seek to provide for the instruction of believers in witnessing to the Gospel.

And they responded:

I affirm.

ॐ

This is an affirmation of responsibility that many evangelists neglect. They recognize their role as spiritual harvesters, but do little, if anything, to preserve the results of their ministries. They may accept that new Christians need to be nurtured, but are quite content to leave this to others. While it is true that other mature Christians will almost certainly have a part in this, the evangelist should not assume that it happens automatically. Converts (or "inquirers" as we call them) need encouragement and instruction from him. Evangelism is more than simply encouraging decisions for Christ. It is urging people to become disciples — followers — of Jesus Christ. As such, the evangelist has a responsibility to make growth in discipleship possible for those who come to faith under his ministry.

In the case of many evangelists, this takes teamwork. When I use the word "evangelist," I am thinking of the team that may travel with the evangelist — be it one or several.

At this point I would also like to mention that I do not think an evangelist should go out alone. Jesus sent them out two by two; and the pattern in the book of Acts was the same. Sometimes they went by threes, fours, or even more. God has given me a team, and there are those who do the preparation, those who do the follow-up. Naturally one man has a difficult time doing it all, especially as he gets older and doesn't have the physical stamina. Therefore responsibility should be delegated to one or more persons who travel with the evangelist.

Parents do not abandon a baby at birth, but nourish and protect the life of the child. So evangelists are to assume responsibility for those born into the family of God under their ministry. The apostle Paul spoke firmly and directly to the Corinthians about his paternal relationship with them. They had many instructors but Paul had a fatherly concern for them that other pastors and teachers did not possess (1 Corinthians 4:14-15). He maintained an active correspondence with them about how they should live, serve, and teach in their church. Paul, as the human instrument who led them into God's family, looked beyond short-term results to growth, maturity, and true reproduction.

To the Colossian church he wrote, "As ye have therefore received Christ Jesus the Lord, so walk ye in him: Rooted and built up in him, and stablished in the faith, as ye have been taught" (Colossians 2:6-7).

Preparation for follow-up begins long before "drawing in the net." Evangelists need to prepare in advance to ensure the spiritual nurture of converts. It is not enough to "leave the results to God" and neglect the care of new Christians. They need help to feed on the Word, walk by faith, and mature in their spiritual life. Paul described his ministry to the Thessalonian converts as that of a nurse who affectionately, gently, and faithfully cares for her children (see 1 Thessalonians 2:7).

Peter used the same picture when he wrote, "As newborn babes, desire the sincere milk of the word, that ye may grow thereby" (1 Peter 2:2).

New converts may suffer from spiritual starvation if we neglect them. Others can be vulnerable to the false teaching of sects or other religions. The evangelistic effort of reaching them is probably just a fraction of what is needed to continue "teaching them to observe all things whatsoever I have commanded you" (Matthew 28:20).

But it's worth it. By providing for new inquirers in this way, the ministry of the evangelist can be multiplied as they learn to teach others (2 Timothy 2:2).

Some inquirers are already in a church. Some have pastors and counselors to minister to them. The evangelist still retains a measure of responsibility for them in two ways.

First, we are responsible to prepare pastors and people before the evangelistic effort. In single church meetings this may involve a preparatory visit which not only encourages a sense of expectancy but prepares the local body of believers to conserve the results. In multi-church efforts special meetings should be held for all the pastors and Christian leaders involved. Where there are no churches in which to place inquirers, some kind of continuing fellowship and perhaps even the planting of a new church should be carefully borne in mind. The harvest must be preserved. This is the apostolic example.

Some churches never seem ready for evangelism. No church is ever ready enough. Sometimes the enthusiasm for evangelism must be created and encouraged. Certainly churches are strengthened and grow spiritually when evangelism is stressed. Evangelism unites, revives, renews, and encourages churches.

Second, under certain circumstances it may be appropriate for the evangelist to prepare materials on discipleship. Perhaps a correspondence course in basic biblical truths would be helpful — especially for isolated inquirers. Maybe one or more follow-up visits could be arranged. Paul did this by the letters he wrote and by returning to instruct and strengthen the believers (e.g., Acts 16:1-5). On occasions, the apostle would leave one of his evangelistic team behind to continue establishing the work begun (e.g., Titus 1:5).

I would not recommend leaving an organization or a person behind for more than a few weeks in an area where there are a number of cooperating churches. Some evangelists have left organizations behind that have undermined a great deal of the good that they did while in the city.

However, I am speaking of areas of the world where there are few or no churches. There may not be an evangelical church within a number of miles. In places like this serious thought should be given to establishing a church. For example, we held meetings a few years ago in southern Mexico. After the meetings a large number of new churches were started, but it was in an area in which the number of churches was relatively small. This has happened in various countries to which we have gone. However, in Great Britain or the United States, for example, we would never think of starting a church or encourage the starting of a church. We would never think of establishing a new parachurch organization in a city as a result of our crusades. We make a promise to pastors that we are there to help them, and serve and strengthen their local churches, not to divide and not to build a competitive organization. In this way the integrity of the evangelist is evidenced, and the confidence of the pastors in the evangelist can be strengthened.

As a further extension of an evangelist's ministry, he should do all he can "to provide for the instruction of believers in witnessing to the gospel." Often the most effective witness to the Gospel is someone who has just discovered the joy of life in Christ. We need to challenge young Christians to share their faith and teach them what the Gospel is in simple terms so they can do this effectively.

For example, look at the woman Jesus encountered at the well, as recorded in John 4. After she had come to know Christ, she went back to her city and announced to the whole community, "Come, see a man, which told me all things that ever I did: is not this the Christ? Then they went out of the city, and came unto him" (John 4:29–30). This woman had been converted only a few hours and she was already an evangelist. The excitement, thrill, and joy of finding Christ spilled over into an entire city. In verse 39 we read, "And many of the Samaritans of that city believed on him for the saying of the woman, which testified." As a result of that woman, Jesus stayed two more days and ministered to the people; and in verse 41 we read that "many more believed because of his own word." This woman introduced an entire city to Jesus Christ even though she had known Christ only a short time. She was doing the work of an evangelist. Sometimes the greatest work of evangelism can be done by a new convert.

I remember when we used to hold very long Crusades; for example, twelve weeks in London, or sixteen weeks in New York — and most of our Crusades were at least six weeks long. The people who accepted Christ in the earlier part of the crusade became evangelists and brought their friends to Christ during the balance of the Crusade! There is no greater witness to Christ than a new convert who is bubbling over with the joy of the Lord. This is the "first love" which so many older Christians seem to lose.

Affirmation XIV

I read aloud the Affirmation:

We share Christ's deep concern for the personal and social sufferings of humanity, and we accept our responsibility as Christians and as evangelists to do our utmost to alleviate human need.

And they responded:

I affirm.

Often I am asked about the relationship between social action and evangelism. While evangelism has priority, social action and evangelism go hand in hand. We must have a burden for the needs of people that goes beyond just "concern" and results in action. We must take a strong stand for racial understanding. We must do something about world hunger. We must work and pray for world peace even when nations arm themselves to the teeth and get ready for Armageddon. *We must* — because God in His love is concerned about every aspect of human suffering.

Some of the greatest social movements in history have been the fruit of true evangelical revival led by the preaching of God-anointed evangelists.

A bishop of the Church of England once told me that he did not know of one great social movement in his country that did not have its roots in some evangelical awakening — resulting from evangelistic preaching.

Where missionaries went around the world carrying the message of Christ's redeeming love, hospitals were built; schools, orphanages, and leprosariums were established; and hundreds of other good works followed.

James 2:14–16 is a good Scripture portion to put all this in perspective. And note how it says of Abraham, that his faith and his actions were working together, "and by works was faith made perfect" (James 2:22).

John writes, "But whoso hath this world's good, and seeth his brother have need, and shutteth up his bowels of compassion from him, how dwelleth the love of God in him? My little children, let us not love in word, neither in tongue; but in deed and in truth" (1 John 3:17–18).

The apostle Paul wrote some of his most impassioned instructions and admonitions on the subject of financial giving to the Corinthian church, in the eighth and ninth chapters of his second letter. I like the way *The Living Bible* renders 2 Corinthians 9:13 on what happens as a result of giving material help, "Those you help will be glad not only because of your generous gifts to themselves and to others, but they will praise God for this proof that your deeds are as good as your doctrine" (TLB).

Christ came to reverse the effects of the Fall. He made it possible for man to have peace with God. This establishing of a vertical relationship inevitably brings into focus the horizontal dimension of our relationship with others. Jesus Himself provided the example when He not only forgave sins but fed the hungry and healed the sick. We must be concerned with human suffering wherever it is found because God is concerned about it.

Evangelists often see people simply as "souls to be saved." But people don't see themselves that way. They need to be met at their perceived point of need. Spurgeon once said, "If you want to give a tract to a hungry man, wrap it in a sandwich!" And sometimes that is the best way to approach someone — touching them first with an expression of our compassion.

There should be no question that God loves the people He created in His own image (Genesis 1:27; Colossians 1:16–17). In His earthly ministry Jesus had compassion on the multitudes around Him. They were harassed and helpless, with no one to care for them (Matthew 9:32–36). Our Lord touched the leper — one who was considered an outcast by society in that time (Matthew 8:1–4). Can you imagine how that leper felt when he was touched? Jesus was teaching by example as well as precept that we have a responsibility to the oppressed, the sick, and the poor. In caring for them Jesus also taught that those who inherit eternal life are to express love for their neighbors in practical ways. He told the story of the Good Samaritan (Luke 10:25–37). Peter was able to point out to Cornelius that Jesus "went about doing good" and was a benefit to others because "God was with him" (Acts 10:38).

Jesus did not reach out and help everyone in need around Him. I don't know all the reasons for that — but perhaps one reason was to show us that even when we can't do *everything*, by God's grace and with His help, we can do *something*. We may feel so overwhelmed by the magnitude of the needs around us that we give up before we begin to help. But we Christians should do what we can to help the poor, to heal the sick, and feed the hungry — although we must never forget that how or when a man dies is less important than where he will spend eternity. If you feed all the hungry and care for all the poor and heal all the sick, yet fail to explain God's way of salvation to them, you have not reached their deepest need. Their deepest need is spiritual.

Others without the motivation of Christian compassion are sometimes involved in helping their fellow human beings. But the Christian goes into the world with an extra dimension in his social concern. We go in the name of our Lord Jesus Christ.

Let's give, but give in Jesus' name. Let's feed, but feed in Jesus' name. Let's heal, but heal in Jesus' name.

That does not mean these issues should form the whole scope of our ministry, nor even be our primary work (although some may be called to specific ministries in this area). While Jesus was deeply concerned about physical and material needs of people, it was the spiritual need and eternal destiny of mankind which dominated His ministry. By His healing power He established His redemptive authority. Healing a paralytic, He said, ''Arise ... and walk'' (Mark 2:9). He did this ''that ye may know that the Son of man hath power on earth to forgive sons'' (Mark 2:10).

The miracle of healing was a bridge, a gracious act which authenticated Jesus' person and power. Today God may similarly use the gifts of His people as ''bridges of love'' to the physically and spiritually needy.

Only the life, death, and resurrection of Jesus authenticates the Gospel, but our lives must reflect this by our social concern and loving service. That's why we are commanded to ''let your light so shine before men, that they may see your good works, and glorify your Father which is in heaven'' (Matthew 5:16). And right after the well-known Scripture which tells us, ''for by grace are ye saved through faith ... Not of works'' (Ephesians 2:8–9), we are reminded that once we are redeemed of God, we are ''created in Christ Jesus unto good works'' (Ephesians 2:10).

The first priority of the church's mission is evangelism. This is our primary concern as evangelists. But just as Paul took time to help the suffering, famine-stricken believers in Judea (Acts 11:27–30), so he encouraged others to "do good unto all men, especially unto them who are of the household of faith" (Galatians 6:10).

This affirmation reminds us that we are to do what we can for the physical and social needs — not only of those we seek to reach with the Gospel — but those of "the family of believers" who are suffering.

Perhaps the most telling incentive to compassionate action came from Jesus Himself after He told the parable of the talents. He spoke of the King saying to the redeemed, "Come, ye blessed of my Father, inherit the kingdom prepared for you from the foundation of the world: For I was an hungred, and ye gave me meat: I was thirsty, and ye gave me drink: I was a stranger, and ye took me in: Naked, and ye clothed me: I was sick, and ye visited me: I was in prison, and ye came unto me.

"Then shall the righteous answer him, saying, Lord, when saw we thee an hungred, and fed thee? or thirsty, and gave thee drink? When saw we thee a stranger, and took thee in? or naked, and clothed thee? Or when saw we thee sick, or in prison, and came unto thee?

"And the King shall answer and say unto them, Verily I say unto you, Inasmuch as ye have done it unto one of the least of these my brethren, ye have done it unto me?" (Matthew 25:34–40).

Our concern for the social needs of others may take many different directions in terms of our action, depending on our opportunities and God's leading. Shortly after my conversion I gradually became aware of the problem of racial injustice in the southern part of the United States, where I was born. It was some time, however, before I realized that I not only needed to be concerned about it, but I needed to do something as well. At one of our Crusades in a southern city, in the early 1950s, I physically removed the ropes that had been put up to keep black people in the rear of the building. Some were enraged at my action, but I determined I would never preach to a segregated audience again.

In other areas of social concern — such as a concern for peace, and a burden for those who are hungry in our world — I have likewise grown (and continue to grow) in my awareness (as this Affirmation states) of "Christ's deep concern for the personal and social sufferings of humanity." We must always, of course, be on guard against becoming so involved in political processes and concerns that we are diverted from our primary calling as evangelists (although God may well call some of His people to be involved in government). But let us all "accept our responsibility as Christians and as evangelists to do our utmost to alleviate human need."

There may come times when we must take stands on issues that may be interpreted as political, socialistic, or capitalistic. We need great discernment at this point. I know of one country where the evangelists joined in a violent revolution, thinking that they were doing the right thing. They did not realize that at the heart of the revolution was a group of radicals who quickly took over control of the country. Now the evangelicals feel that they have jumped from the frying pan into the fire. Whereas before they at least had liberty in proclaiming the Gospel, now that liberty is greatly curtailed. And many of their church activities have been cut off. Therefore we need a great deal of prayer and discernment in taking these stands. Let's be sure that we are "in the will of God," remembering that no social structure or political structure is absolutely perfect. Sometimes we just substitute one group of sinners for another group of sinners.

Affirmation XV

---⚘---

I read publicly the following Affirmation:

We beseech the Body of Christ to join with us in prayer and work for peace in our world, for revival and a renewed dedication to the biblical priority of evangelism in the church, and for the oneness of believers in Christ for the fulfillment of the Great Commission, until Christ returns.

Four thousand itinerant evangelists replied audibly:

I affirm.

---⚘---

The final Affirmation is an appeal to the Body of Christ, the people of God, the church throughout the world. It is an urgent request for a renewed partnership in prayer and work. It looks, therefore, to the time when all believers will grasp anew a clear vision of God's purposes for this world and commit themselves to pray and work with all their energy to accomplish God's will.

In this Affirmation the first appeal to the Body of

Christ is "to join with us in prayer and work for peace in our world." Psalm 34:14 commands us to "seek peace, and pursue it" — a verse that is repeated in 1 Peter 3:11. Zechariah 8:19 says, "Love the truth and peace." Jesus, the Prince of Peace, declared to His disciples, "Blessed are the peacemakers: for they shall be called the children of God" (Matthew 5:9). Paul stated to the young pastor Timothy, "I exhort therefore, that, first of all, supplications, prayers, intercessions, and giving of thanks, be made for all men; for kings, and for all that are in authority; that we may lead a quiet and peaceable life in all godliness and honesty. For this is good and acceptable in the sight of God our Savior" (1 Timothy 2:1-3).

The Bible speaks of three kinds of peace. First, there is *peace with God*, which is possible because of what God has done in Jesus Christ. "Therefore being justified by faith, we have peace with God through our Lord Jesus Christ" (Romans 5:1). Second, there is the *peace of God* in our hearts. This peace is more than a human contentment which comes when circumstances are congenial. This is the peace which comes when we know that our sins are forgiven and that God is with us every moment of the day. "But the fruit of the Spirit is . . . peace" (Galatians 5:22). Third, there is *peace between man and man*, and between nations. The ancient Hebrew prophets pleaded with the leaders and people of Israel to repent and turn back to God. Why? One reason is that they knew that war and devastation would come upon the nation if they did not repent, and they wanted to do all in their power to avert such a catastrophe. Isaiah's vision of the messianic kingdom vividly illustrates God's burden for peace between men and nations: "And he shall judge among the nations, and shall rebuke many people: and they shall beat their swords into plowshares, and their spears into pruninghooks: nation shall not lift up sword against nation, neither shall they learn war any more" (Isaiah 2:4).

Peace with God — the peace of God — the peace of men and nations with each other — God is concerned about all three kinds of peace. And so must we be. No true and lasting world peace will come until Christ returns and sets up His kingdom. But that does not excuse us from our responsibility to pray and work for peace — any more than the fact that not all men will become believers gives us an excuse to quit preaching the Gospel.

How we carry out this responsibility will differ according to our opportunities and our calling. The issue of peace in our world today is often extremely complex, with difficult and complicated political dimensions. We must avoid the temptation to propose simplistic solutions that might result in the long run in even greater evils. I am not for unilateral disarmament, nor am I a pacifist; I believe a legitimate government has a right to defend itself.

But the church is to do all it possibly can, in accordance with its spiritual mission and its call under God, to be an instrument of peace. We must bring the Gospel of peace with God to those who do not know Christ. We must be channels through whom God brings His peace to the hearts of men. And we must be instruments of His peace in our torn and fear-filled world. God is a God of peace in the heart, in the home, in the church, in the community, in the nation and the world. In the midst of a world that seems to be tottering on the brink of a man-made nuclear or biochemical Armageddon, let us (in the words of this Affirmation) ''beseech the Body of Christ to join with us in prayer and work for peace in our world.''

The second appeal in this final Affirmation is for ''the Body of Christ to join with us in prayer and work . . . for revival and a renewed dedication to the biblical priority of evangelism in the church.'' The greatest need for God's people today is true spiritual revival — a fresh outpouring of the Holy Spirit on the church, a profound repentance and turning from sin, and a deepening commitment to God's will in every area of life. The Bible promises, "If my people, which are called by my name, shall humble themselves, and pray, and seek my face, and turn from their wicked ways; then will I hear from heaven, and will forgive their sin, and will heal their land" (2 Chronicles 7:14).

Revival and evangelism are not the same. Revival is concerned with the renewal of God's people; evangelism is concerned with those who have never known Christ. But the two are intimately connected. When God's people are truly revived and renewed spiritually, it results in a new vision for a lost world and a new commitment to reach out to those who do not belong to Christ. Evangelism is the fruit of revival among God's people. If we have little interest in reaching our world for Christ, it shows that the work of revival (or renewal) needs to begin in our own hearts.

Revival has to do with Christians. It involves the confession and forsaking of sins which grieve the Holy Spirit, hinder peace in the church, and joy in the lives of God's people. In preparation of evangelism, revival is essential. It enables Christians to grow spiritually and gives them an incentive to work and share their faith. Newborn babies thrive best in an atmosphere of warmth, nourishment, love, and peace. So the spirit of revival (or renewal) in a church makes a good environment for those brought to Christ through evangelistic outreach.

We should pray and work for revival, and we must also pray and work (in the words of the Affirmation) for "a renewed dedication to the biblical priority of evangelism in the church." God's people are called by God to do various things. We are called to worship God. We are called to teach the Word of God so that believers might be strengthened. We are called to have a social concern for those in need in our world. All of these responsibilities (and others we might mention) are legitimate and important. But the greatest responsibility — the highest priority — is evangelism, reaching a lost world for Christ.

Tragically, the church has often lost sight of this, relegating evangelism to the status of a minor program, or even redefining evangelism so that the biblical mandate and message are lost. We should be thankful for evidences today of a renewed commitment to evangelism by many churches — but we should also be concerned that other parts of the Body of Christ have become indifferent to the plight of the lost and have become preoccupied with internal programs. May those of us to whom God has entrusted a special ministry of evangelism be burdened for God's people, and pray and work for a restoration of the biblical priority of evangelism to the church of Jesus Christ, in all of its diversity around the world.

The third appeal of this final Affirmation is for "the Body of Christ to join with us in prayer and work . . . for the oneness of believers in Christ for the fulfillment of the Great Commission, until Christ returns." Christ prayed concerning His disciples "that they all may be one; as thou, Father, art in me, and I in thee." Then Christ gave the reason for this petition, "that the world may believe that thou hast sent me" (John 17:21).

Unity of Christians is a biblical objective. Does this mean that we should all be part of the same external organization: No, this is not necessarily the case. At times, of course, organizational unity may be God's will and should be pursued; often our divisions are caused by pride and a wrongful lust for power or petty church politics rather than a concern to do God's work. But we can become preoccupied with organizational unity and lose sight of the true spiritual unity of which Jesus speaks.

Christians may disagree on minor issues and traditions. But they are united on one thing: the Gospel of Jesus Christ. That is why the proclamation of the simple Gospel of Christ often unites believers in a way that nothing else ever can. I have seen evangelism unite believers within a church, and among churches of different backgrounds, in a way that no high-level appeal for unity has ever managed to do. Evangelism exalts Jesus Christ. Evangelism encourages personal and united witness. Evangelism causes the church to grow spiritually, numerically, and geographically. I recall a Lutheran bishop in Hungary saying, "The closer we get to Christ, the closer we get to one another." That is true. There is joy in heaven that is reflected in the joy of believers as God's people unite in obedience to the Great Commission.

I have seen that one of the great side-effects of our crusades is the way in which this common objective of evangelism brings Christians together. Sometimes they live in the same city but have never worked together before. Time after time we hear them say, "I wish we'd learned to work together like this years ago!" The story is told of two sailors who were fighting fiercely on the upper deck of a ship. Suddenly they heard another sailor shout, "Man overboard!" Without a moment's hesitation, both the fighting men plunged into the sea to rescue the drowning man. When they surfaced, both were helping the man in need! Fighting each other divided them; saving a drowning man united them!

One vital aspect of our unity with other believers in the task of evangelism should be a true partnership in prayer — especially prayer for our work of evangelism. Evangelism is the central mission of the church. Without it, believers become introspective and lacking in purpose, growth stagnates, worship becomes superficial, and selfishness stifles a spirit of giving. If evangelism is so vital to the life of the church, those set apart to "do the work of an evangelist" deserve prayer support.

Jesus wanted His disciples to stay awake during His decisive prayer-battle in the Garden of Gethsemane. The apostle Paul sought the prayers of the churches for his evangelistic ministry. To the Roman church he wrote, "Now I beseech you, brethren, for the Lord Jesus Christ's sake, and for the love of the Spirit, that ye strive together with me in your prayers to God for me" (Romans 15:30). The Ephesian church was requested to pray "for me, that utterance may be given unto me, that I may open my mouth boldly, to make known the mystery of the gospel" (Ephesians 6:19). Of the Colossian church he asked, "[Pray] also for us, that God would open unto us a door of utterance" (Colossians 4:3).

Prayer for evangelism and evangelists is important and essential. It is a means by which the whole church can share in the completion of the Great Commission throughout the whole world. Prayer is hard work and should be rewarded by reports from the evangelists who are prayed for. In this way those who are faithful in prayer can be encouraged.

Finally, we look in this Affirmation to the promise of Christ's return. When He does, our task of evangelism and the mission of the church will be completed. The apostles had the great privilege of being the first generation of Christians to whom Jesus gave that Great Commission. Today's worldwide church is a testimony to the fact that they took the commission seriously. Against tremendous odds, in the power of the Holy Spirit, they tackled a humanly impossible task of evangelism. But their God is our God, and by the same Holy Spirit we are linked to the vast resources of His power.

As the apostles were the first generation of evangelists, we may be the last before Jesus returns. The signs could well indicate this.

"And there shall be signs in the sun, and in the moon, and in the stars; and upon the earth distress of nations, with perplexity; ... Men's hearts failing them for fear, and for looking after those things which are coming on the earth: ... And then shall they see the Son of man coming in a cloud with power and great glory. And when these things begin to come to pass, then look up, and lift up your heads; for your redemption draweth nigh'' (Luke 21:25-28).

This is the Christian's blessed hope.

''For the Son of man shall come in the glory of his Father with his angels; and then he shall reward every man according to his works'' (Matthew 16:27).

Yes, God has a plan for the future. Today there are all types of political philosophies and ideologies that compete for the loyalty of men. Each of them promises a bright, trouble-free future. But even the best of them cannot make the world a perfect place, because they are powerless to deal with the ultimate problem which is at the root of all other problems: the selfishness and sin of the human heart. Only Christ can change the human heart, and only Christ can establish a kingdom of true justice. And some day Christ's kingdom will come in all its fullness. ''Nevertheless we, according to his promise, look for new heavens and a new earth, wherein dwelleth righteousness'' (2 Peter 3:13).

God has a plan for this planet. Some day when man and human society reach a point when it looks as if the human race is doomed, God will intervene and Jesus Christ will come back as King of kings and Lord of lords. He will return in triumph and glory to establish His eternal kingdom; and the vision of John in Revelation 11:15 will be fulfilled, ''And the seventh angel sounded; and there were great voices in heaven, saying, The kingdoms of this world are become the kingdoms of our Lord, and of his Christ; and he shall reign for ever and ever.''

When that glorious day comes, sin and death will be destroyed and Satan will be banished. All the strife and hatred and suffering and death that twist and scar this world will vanish, and the Lord's Prayer will be fulfilled: God's will *will* be done on earth as it is in heaven. In that day the words of Revelation will be a reality, ''Behold, the tabernacle of God is with men, and he will dwell with them, and they shall be his people, and God himself shall be with them, and be their God. And God shall wipe away all tears from their eyes; and there shall be no more death, neither sorrow, nor crying, neither shall there be any more pain: for the former things are passed away. And he that sat upon the throne said, Behold, I make all things new'' (Revelation 21:3–5). This is our hope!

Our world today desperately hungers for hope, and yet uncounted people have almost given up. There is despair and hopelessness on every hand. Let us be faithful in proclaiming the hope that is in Jesus! We need to preach more often on the subject of the Second Coming. I find that few sermons are preached today on the subject of the Second Coming, and that is unfortunate. Those of us who are evangelists especially need to point people to the only hope there is for a better world and for life after death — the blessed hope of Christ and His kingdom.

But the Second Coming of Christ also reminds us of another sobering fact.

We do not know when Christ will come, for ''of that day and hour knoweth no man, no, not the angels of heaven, but my Father only'' (Matthew 24:36). But when He comes again, it will be too late to call people to follow Christ. It will be too late for men and women to hear the Gospel and turn to Christ for salvation. If ever we are going to serve Christ, it must be *now*. If ever we are to proclaim the Gospel, it must be *now*. ''I must work the works of him that sent me, while it is day: the night cometh, when no man can work'' (John 9:4).

We do not know when Christ may return — but what if it were today? Would Christ find you working for Him? Would He find you living a life of holiness that honored Him? Would He find you doing all you could to share the glorious Gospel of salvation with others who do not know Him? ''Seeing then that all these things shall be dissolved, what manner of persons ought ye to be in all holy conversation and godliness, Looking for and hasting unto the coming of the day of God, ... Wherefore, beloved, seeing that ye look for such things, be diligent that ye may be found of him in peace, without spot, and blameless" (2 Peter 3:11-12,14).

In light of all that Christ has done for us — in light of His call to us — in light of all that He will do some day when He returns, let us as evangelists be faithful in our proclamation of the Gospel of Jesus Christ. This is the commission God has given to His church, and it is the priority He has given especially to those of us who are called to be evangelists. Let us never lose sight of that urgent task.

During recent decades we have seen tools developed which would have been unimaginable to evangelists in other generations — jet travel, films, radio and television, video and audio cassettes — the list is almost endless. With the aid of modern technology we can go farther and reach more people with the Gospel than ever before.

But technology alone is insufficient. Strategies alone are not enough. More than anything else, God requires men and women who will give themselves without reserve as living sacrifices (Romans 12:1-2), in response to the challenge Jesus gave when He said, "As my Father hath sent me, even so send I you" (John 20:21).

There is no higher calling and privilege than to be a part of God's plan for evangelism in the world today. There also is no greater responsibility. May nothing — no matter how enticing or how noble — divert us from God's calling.

John R. Mott was perhaps the greatest and most respected missionary statesman in the early decades of the twentieth century. From his vision and work came the 1910 Edinburgh Conference which gave the great impetus to missions and evangelism under its slogan, "The Evangelization of the World in This Generation." He also has been called the father of the ecumenical movement because of his work to bring churches together from various traditions in order to make them more effective in their evangelistic task. When John Mott was in his eighties, he was introduced at a major church conference and invited to say something. After the prolonged applause had died down, he slowly rose to his feet and simply said in a ringing voice, "Let it always be said that John R. Mott was an evangelist!" Then he sat down.

Let it be said that we too were evangelists — that we were faithful to the call of God to go and preach the Gospel! Let us not be concerned about the praise — or even the undeserved criticism — of men, but let us be supremely concerned about the will and the approval of God.

And some day Christ will come again in all His glory. Then we will know in a fuller and far deeper way that whatever sacrifices we might have made for Christ's sake were nothing compared with His sacrifice for us, and the glory of heaven. "For our light affliction, which is but for a moment, worketh for us a far more exceeding and eternal weight of glory; while we look not at the things which are seen, but at the things which are not seen: for the things which are seen are temporal; but the things which are not seen are eternal" (2 Corinthians 4:17-18).

"He which testifieth these things saith, Surely I come quickly. Amen. Even so, come, Lord Jesus" (Revelation 22:20).

But, until that day, let us with confidence claim that glorious benediction recorded by the apostle Paul in 1 Thessalonians 5:23-24:

> "And the very God of peace sanctify you wholly; and I pray God your whole spirit and soul and body be preserved blameless unto the coming of our Lord Jesus Christ. Faithful is he that calleth you, who also will do it."